HOPE
ETERNAL

HOPE ETERNAL

Encouraging
Words for
Discouraging
Times

~

S E L W Y N   H U G H E S

BROADMAN
& HOLMAN
PUBLISHERS

Nashville, Tennessee

Includes the complete text of
Your Personal Encourager by Selwyn Hughes
British edition copyright © 1994 by CWR
Used by permission

0–8054–1767–2

Published by Broadman & Holman Publishers, Nashville, Tennessee
Acquisitions & Development Editor: Leonard G. Goss
Interior Design: Anderson Thomas Design
Typesetting: TF Designs, Mt. Juliet, Tennessee

Subject Heading: DEVOTIONAL EXERCISES

Unless otherwise stated all Scripture citation is from
the Holy Bible, New International Version,
copyright © 1973, 1978, 1984 by International Bible Society.
Other versions used are marked KJV, the King James Version;
and NKJV, the New King James Version,
copyright © 1979, 1980, 1982, Thomas Nelson, Inc., Publishers.

1 2 3 4 5 02 01 00 99 98

May our
Lord Jesus Christ himself
and God our Father,
who loved us and by his grace
gave us eternal encouragement
and good hope,
encourage your hearts
and strengthen you
in every good deed and word.

2 Thessalonians 2:16–17

~

CONTENTS

From time to time everyone needs encouragement. In all the years I have been a counselor—now over forty—I have met only a few people who didn't respond positively to a few carefully chosen and biblically based words of encouragement. Some of the most remembered moments in my own life have been when I was overtaken by a pressing problem and feeling deeply discouraged, and someone came alongside and stimulated my faith with a God-given and reassuring word.

The word *discourage* means "to deprive of courage, to dishearten, to deter." Almost every day we face discouraging circumstances and situations: a put-down from someone, a critical word, plans that don't seem to work out, loneliness, sorrow, failure, doubts, and so on. The word *encourage*, in contrast, means "to inspire with new confidence and courage, to give spirit or hope, to hearten, to spur on, to give help." A Christian once told me: "I can go for a whole month on a single word of encouragement."

Friends are fine (thank God for them), but we must know for ourselves how to think biblically about life's problems, to talk to ourselves about the facts of our faith, and then find the appropriate Scriptures that relate to our problem.

It is imperative that we know which parts of the Bible to turn to in times of testing, and also that we know how to talk ourselves into a new mood of optimism and faith. The things we tell ourselves greatly affect the way we feel—and this is why we must learn to fill our minds with the truths of God's eternal and unchanging Word.

I can't emphasize strongly enough that our negative self-talk is often responsible for the way we feel. We talk ourselves into a low mood by repeating statements to ourselves that either minimize or maximize the facts. And just as we talk ourselves into downcast feelings, so we can talk ourselves out of them. Over the years in which I have been involved in Christian counseling I have often asked people the question: What discourages you? I have taken the hundreds of replies I have received and narrowed them down to the forty most oft-repeated issues. If your particular problem does not fall within these categories then look for the one that comes closest to it. I feel confident you will find something that will revive, refresh, and minister to your spirit.

You can use *Hope Eternal* in two ways: (1) to help you find the relevant Scriptures and thoughts you need to consider when overtaken by some aspect of discouragement; and (2) to help you minister to others when they need encouragement.

It goes without saying that the power of this publication lies in the words of Scripture that it highlights and identifies. I have also given some explanations and statements of my own, together with a prayer that can be used at the end. If you do not find the prayer helpful, then compile your own. I am sure it hardly needs to be said that my comments are of much lesser value than the words of Scripture. But they are based on Scripture and built around such great themes as God's sovereignty, power, compassion, and forgiveness. The thoughts and ideas recorded here have been used in countless counseling situations over the years. Many people have told me they have found them helpful. I hope you will too.

One final thing: encouragement must not be regarded as mere sentimentality. We should realize that Scripture is equally encouraging when it confronts and challenges us as it is when it consoles and comforts us. To be faced with a challenge when we are hurting may not be what we most want, but it may be what we most need. An African tribe says of medicine that is not too pleasing to the taste but does them good: "It hurts better." Keep in mind that when God challenges us it is only that we might be brought to the place of complete dependency upon him. God not only lifts the standards to great heights, but also provides the power to reach up to them.

Personally, I find it deeply encouraging that God thinks so much of me that he will not let me get away with things that could damage my potential and hinder my effectiveness for him. He loves me as I am, but he loves me too much to let me stay as I am. So remember it is still the ministry of encouragement that is at work when Scripture speaks to us in a challenging and confronting way. See these as the Lord's "loving reproofs," for that is just what they are.

May you learn the skill of encouraging yourself in the Lord your God.

Selwyn Hughes
Waverley Abbey House
Farnham, Surrey, England

WHEN BETRAYED BY A FRIEND ─────────

—The closer the friendship, the deeper the hurt.
If an enemy were insulting me, I could endure it; if a foe were raising himself against me, I could hide from him. But it is you, a man like myself, my companion, my close friend, with whom I once enjoyed sweet fellowship as we walked with the throng at the house of God. (Ps. 55:12–14)

—Our Lord knew betrayal also.
While he was still speaking . . . one of the Twelve . . . approached Jesus to kiss him, but Jesus asked him, "Judas, are you betraying the Son of Man with a kiss?" (Luke 22:47–48)

—Betrayal is a universal and age-old problem.
For a son dishonors his father, a daughter rises up against her mother, a daughter-in-law against her mother-in-law—a man's enemies are the members of his own household. (Mic. 7:6)

—Transfer all ideas of vengeance to God.
Do not take revenge, my friends, but leave room for God's wrath, for it is written: "It is mine to avenge; I will repay," says the Lord. (Rom. 12:19)

—Let God restore your soul.
He makes me lie down in green pastures, he leads me beside quiet waters, he restores my soul. (Ps. 23:2–3a)

—Don't hit back.
Do not repay evil with evil or insult with insult, but with blessing, because to this you were called so that you may inherit a blessing. (1 Pet. 3:9)

—See how much you have been forgiven.
Bear with each other and forgive whatever grievances you may have against one another. Forgive as the Lord forgave you. (Col. 3:13)

—Jesus forgave; he can help you forgive too.
Jesus said, "Father, forgive them, for they do not know what they are doing." (Luke 23:34)

1

There is a terrible sound in the word *betrayed*. To betray someone is to deal treacherously with that person. Betrayal is the opposite of loyalty, and the more we love loyalty the more we loathe betrayal. In a hard and cruel world such as this we are not surprised when we are hurt by our enemies, but no one expects to be hurt by a friend. Few things, I imagine, hurt our Lord more than when he was betrayed by one of his own disciples. How do we cope with betrayal? How do we handle our lives when we become a victim of treachery by a friend?

First, we must take our pain to God and invite him to invade our hearts with his soothing balm. Who better than Jesus can sympathize with us in this kind of problem? It is perilously easy to turn elsewhere for comfort in such an hour—alcohol, entertainment, literature, and so on. Some even attempt to push the matter out of awareness. But all painful situations must be faced, even though they do not have to be dwelt upon. We must let God minister to us in our hurt; he is the only one who can restore the soul.

Because hurt can quickly escalate into resentment, with the help of our Lord we must empty our hearts of all bitterness—and forgive. Forgiveness, it must be understood, may not always bring about changes in the other person (nor guarantee that he or she will want to be restored), but it will ensure release for our own souls.

The cross of our Lord Jesus Christ stands and holds out wide, appealing arms to all who have been betrayed. It says: "This is how Jesus dealt with his enemies . . . *and* the friend who betrayed him." In the light of that great fact, can we do anything other than forgive?

> *Father, give me the grace to follow your example in the midst of my betrayal. Show me that nothing—not even betrayal by a friend—can move my soul from its security in you. May I rejoice in that and in the power of your great love. Amen.*

WHEN BETRAYED BY A FRIEND

WHEN GOD SEEMS FAR AWAY ―――――

―We just can't get away from God.
Where can I go from your Spirit? Where can I flee from your presence? If I go up to the heavens, you are there; if I make my bed in the depths, you are there. If I rise on the wings of the dawn, if I settle on the far side of the sea, even there your hand will guide me, your right hand will hold me fast. (Ps. 139:7–10)

―God may seem far away, but actually he is not.
God did this so that men would seek him and perhaps reach out for him and find him, though he is not far from each one of us. "For in him we live and move and have our being." As some of your own poets have said, "We are his offspring." (Acts 17:27–28)

―God cannot go back on his Word.
If we are faithless, he will remain faithful, for he cannot disown himself. (2 Tim. 2:13)

―Never means never.
God has said, "Never will I leave you; never will I forsake you." (Heb. 13:5b)

―God sustains us even when we don't realize it.
My flesh and my heart may fail, but God is the strength of my heart and my portion forever. (Ps. 73:26)

―If we really want to find him, God can be found.
"You will seek me and find me when you seek me with all your heart. I will be found by you," declares the LORD. (Jer. 29:13–14)

―There is never a moment when God is not with us.
God is our refuge and strength, an ever-present help in trouble. (Ps. 46:1)

―God pursues his purposes no matter what.
Once you were alienated from God and were enemies in your minds because of your evil behavior. But now he has reconciled you by Christ's physical body through death to present you holy in his sight, without blemish and free from accusation. (Col. 1:21–22)

2

Sometimes even mature Christians who have followed the Lord for many years go through times when God seems very far away. Generally, there are three possible reasons for this.

First, the problem can stem from a purely physical cause. What happens to us physically can have a great effect upon us spiritually. Sickness, viral infections, stress, overwork, or other physical conditions can affect our moods to such a degree that we think we are spiritually low when the real problem is a poor physical condition. This is why, before God began to work on Elijah's depressed spirit, he made sure that he had a period of rest and recuperation (1 Kings 19).

Second, God might seem far away because you haven't repented of a particular sin. God has so built our spiritual system that when we sin, guilt descends. This kind of guilt (as opposed to the false guilt, which can arise in our personalities) is God's way of getting our attention. In this situation repentance is the only way back. Repentance, remember, means more than just being sorry; it means being sorry enough to quit. When repentance has taken effect we can be sure that our relationship with God will be restored.

The third reason—and by far the most common one—for feeling that God is far away is that we fail to take the time to maintain our relationship with him. If we don't take the time to talk to God regularly in prayer and listen to him through reading his Word, then ought it to surprise us that the relationship between us and him begins to deteriorate? As someone put it: "If God seems far away—guess who moved?" God *never* moves away from us; it's we who move away from him.

> My Father and my God, thank you for reminding me
> that my relationship with you must not be taken for
> granted, but constantly maintained. And if repentance
> is what is needed, help me to take that step—and with-
> out delay. In Jesus' name, Amen.

WHEN GOD SEEMS FAR AWAY ———

—Turn your thinking in the right direction.
Finally, brothers, whatever is true, whatever is noble, whatever is right, whatever is pure, whatever is lovely, whatever is admirable—if anything is excellent or praiseworthy—think about such things. (Phil. 4:8)

—God says to all temptation: "so far and no farther."
No temptation has seized you except what is common to man. And God is faithful; he will not let you be tempted beyond what you can bear. But when you are tempted, he will also provide a way out so that you can stand up under it. (1 Cor. 10:13)

—The "hidden" Word—a great resource against evil.
How can a young man keep his way pure? By living according to your word. I seek you with all my heart; do not let me stray from your commands. I have hidden your word in my heart that I might not sin against you. (Ps. 119:9–11)

—Put on the armor of God and feel the difference.
Put on the full armor of God so that you can take your stand against the devil's schemes. (Eph. 6:11)

—A threefold prescription.
Submit yourselves, then, to God. Resist the devil, and he will flee from you. Come near to God and he will come near to you. (James 4:7)

—Decide not to let a glance become a gaze.
I made a covenant with my eyes not to look lustfully at a girl. (Job 31:1)

—Your mind works better when filled with Scripture.
Do not conform any longer to the pattern of this world, but be transformed by the renewing of your mind. Then you will be able to test and approve what God's will is—his good, pleasing and perfect will." (Rom. 12:2)

3

Many Christians are molested by evil thoughts and have to fight a difficult battle in their minds and imaginations. Evil thoughts can vary from wanting to inflict harm on others to horrifying images of sexual lust. The entrance of a wrong thought into the mind is not sin, but if it is not dealt with quickly and efficiently it can soon lead to sin. The longer a thought is indulged the more energy it gathers and the deeper it becomes entrenched in the mind. Note this: *If the battle is lost it is usually lost in the first few minutes.* Thus those who entertain evil thoughts on the pretext that they can dismiss them anytime they like are playing a foolish game.

The path along which an evil thought proceeds takes this form: a thought comes and is indulged, indulging a thought quickly leads to inclination, inclination leads to appetite, appetite leads to hunger, hunger leads to craving, and craving leads to sin. Those afflicted by evil thoughts should be careful about the literature they read, the films they see, and the programs they watch on television. *Avoid all those things that have a tendency to inflame.*

Evil thoughts are not driven out by dwelling on them, but by turning the attention to other subjects. It is bad tactics to give them sustained attention; they must be outwitted at once by directing the mind to a more purifying and absorbing theme. And what better theme than Jesus? He is the center of everything that is pure. To focus on him is to enlist his aid. So the first moment an evil thought assails you, *focus on Jesus*. And as he has been there for others, he will be there also for you.

> O God, help me whenever I find myself in the heat of a
> mental fight to turn my thoughts swiftly to you. May I
> discover how things so seductive apart from you take on
> a loathsome appearance when you are consciously pres-
> ent. In Jesus' name I pray, Amen.

WHEN EVIL THOUGHTS ASSAIL ———

———

~

—Christ's death on the cross related to healing.
When evening came, many who were demon-possessed were brought to him, and he drove out the spirits with a word and healed all the sick. This was to fulfill what was spoken through the prophet Isaiah: "He took up our infirmities and carried our diseases." (Matt. 8:16–17)

—Healing is part of the divine purpose.
I am the LORD, who heals you. (Exod. 15:26)

—Have you done this?
Is any one of you sick? He should call the elders of the church to pray over him and anoint him with oil in the name of the Lord. (James 5:14)

—Healing may not come, but God's strength always does.
He gives strength to the weary
   and increases the power of the weak. (Isa. 40:29)

—Another promise of divine strength.
You are awesome, O God, in your sanctuary; the God of Israel gives power and strength to his people. Praise be to God! (Ps. 68:35)

—All-sufficient grace.
But he said to me, "My grace is sufficient for you, for my power is made perfect in weakness." Therefore I will boast all the more gladly about my weaknesses, so that Christ's power may rest on me. (2 Cor. 12:9)

—Yet more strength.
So do not fear, for I am with you;
   do not be dismayed, for I am your God.
I will strengthen you and help you;
   I will uphold you with my righteous right hand. (Isa. 41:10)

—The comfort God gives you can be used to comfort others.
Who comforts us in all our troubles, so that we can comfort those in any trouble with the comfort we ourselves have received from God. (2 Cor. 1:4)

4

Clearly, the Scriptures reveal that God is able and willing to heal the sickness of his people. He healed men and women in both Old and New Testament times. One of God's Old Testament names is *Jehovah Rophi*, which means: "I am the LORD who heals" (Exod. 15:26). And in the Book of James—one of many New Testament Scriptures on the theme of healing—we are encouraged to pray for one another that we might be healed (James 5:16).

When serious sickness afflicts us we ought to seek all legitimate means of healing, beginning *first* with inviting those who represent the local church to pray over us, anointing us with oil (James 5:14). Medical advice ought to be sought also. It is not lack of faith to seek medical help when sick, even when one has been prayed for by the leaders of the church.

But what happens when sickness continues and healing does not come? God is able to keep us brave when not blithe; aware of his presence even though not abounding with vitality. God does not *always* heal, and no matter how we may rationalize this fact we must see there is an element of mystery about the subject of healing. No one knew or has ever been more conscious of the problem of why God does not always deliver us from our afflictions than God's servant Job. He asked numerous questions of the Almighty but none of them, in fact, was answered. Instead God gave Job something better—*a richer and deeper sense of his presence.*

God may not give us a clear answer as to why we are not healed, but he will, if we let him, give us a richer awareness of himself. Nothing could be more wonderful than that.

> *O God, help me never to lose sight of the fact that you are able to heal. But never let me lose sight also of the truth that when for some reason I am not healed, you draw closer to me than I could possibly have imagined. Do it now, dear Lord. In Jesus' name, Amen.*

WHEN WORN WITH SICKNESS ——————

WHEN FEARS TRANSCEND ─────────

—Why fear when God is who he is?
The LORD is my light and my salvation—
    whom shall I fear?
The LORD is the stronghold of my life—
    of whom shall I be afraid? (Ps. 27:1)

—By fearing God, one need fear nothing else.
Even though I walk through the valley of the shadow of death, I will
fear no evil, for you are with me; your rod and your staff, they comfort me. (Ps. 23:4)

—Trust in God—the only safe position.
Fear of man will prove to be a snare, but whoever trusts in the LORD
is kept safe. (Prov. 29:25)

—Fear is not part of sonship.
For you did not receive a spirit that makes you a slave again to fear,
but you received the Spirit of sonship. And by him we cry, "*Abba*,
Father." (Rom. 8:15)

—God commands us not to fear.
But now, this is what the LORD says—he who created you, O Jacob,
he who formed you, O Israel: "Fear not, for I have redeemed you; I
have summoned you by name; you are mine." (Isa. 43:1)

—The universe may fold up—but God? Never.
God is our refuge and strength,
    an ever-present help in trouble.
Therefore we will not fear, though the earth give way
    and the mountains fall into the heart of the sea. (Ps. 46:1–2)

—The Almighty—a safe and sure Refuge.
The name of the LORD is a strong tower;
    the righteous run to it and are safe. (Prov. 18:10)

—God's peace—a sentinel who never goes off duty.
And the peace of God, which transcends all understanding, will guard
your hearts and your minds in Christ Jesus. (Phil. 4:7)

Fear, it must be said at once, can be a friend as well as a foe. A healthy fear keeps us from rushing across a traffic-congested street; it compels caution and preserves life. An unhealthy fear, however, grows into a bogey in the mind and can quickly enslave the whole personality. The four most common fears in human life (sometimes called "The Fearsome Foursome") are these: (1) the fear of rejection, (2) the fear of failure, (3) the fear of death, and (4) the fear of falling into despair.

How does Christ enable his children to deal with fear? He does it by imparting to us the energy and power to face anything that comes, and giving us the gripping assurance that whatever the difficulties we have to face, we can be more than a match for them—*in him*. The apostle Paul put it like this: "For God did not give us a spirit of timidity, but a spirit of power, of love and of self-discipline" (2 Tim. 1:7).

The one thing that underlies all unhealthy fear is the desire for avoidance. The fearful heart says: "When afraid—avoid." Such is the strengthening of the Holy Spirit's work in our souls, however, that he enables us to face whatever it is that troubles us, knowing that no matter what happens, it can never separate us from God and his unending love. The apostle John said: "Perfect love drives out fear" (1 John 4:18). Resting in God's love—a love that will never let us go— we can move into any situation that makes us afraid with a confidence that transcends all fear. Fear says: "Avoid." Faith says: "Confront." Therefore move with God towards the thing you fear, and just see what God will do.

> O God, with you behind me, in front of me, and within me, whom or what need I fear? When love comes in, fear flies out. I open my heart to your love and ask now that all fear might fly out. In Jesus' name I pray, Amen.

WHEN FEARS TRANSCEND

—No orphans in God's family.
I will not leave you as orphans; I will come to you. (John 14:18)

—Take a step closer to God.
Come near to God and he will come near to you. (James 4:8)

—Those who ask, get.
Then you will call, and the LORD will answer;
   you will cry for help, and he will say: Here am I. (Isa. 58:9)

—God never separates or divorces his people.
I will betroth you to me forever;
I will betroth you in righteousness and justice, in love and compassion. (Hos. 2:19)

—Spend time with God and he will spend time with you.
The LORD confides in those who fear him; he makes his covenant known to them. (Ps. 25:14)

—Concentrate on being a friend.
Share with God's people who are in need. Practice hospitality.
(Rom. 12:13)

—Put others ahead of yourself.
Love must be sincere. Hate what is evil; cling to what is good. Be devoted to one another in brotherly love. Honor one another above yourselves. (Rom. 12:9–10)

—Love—the greatest virtue.
And over all these virtues put on love, which binds them all together in perfect unity. (Col. 3:14)

Loneliness is the feeling we experience when we hunger for human companionship but are bereft of it. It is important, however, to differentiate between loneliness that arises from circumstances beyond our control (when we are shut in by sickness or disability, for example) and loneliness that comes from an inability to relate well to others.

When we are lonely because of life's circumstances we must remember that nothing can interfere with our communion with heaven. Though shut off from others, we can still have contact with the Friend of friends. An elderly Christian man who lived in a home for senior citizens said, "I spend all of my time in this home, but I *live* in God."

Many people, though, are lonely not by reason of their circumstances but because of an inability to relate. In a needy world like ours, it has been said, anyone can have friendship who will give friendship. A very lonely individual became someone who was sought after by many after he heard his pastor say in a sermon, "The best way to have a friend is to be a friend." He went home, got down on his knees, and prayed, "Lord, forgive me for focusing more on myself than others. From now on I will move towards others with the same love by which you move towards me." As his thoughts changed from self-centeredness to other-centeredness he became a more interesting and attractive personality. His circle of friends widened, and he became outgoing in all his relationships.

No Christian is ever without the friendship of God, but when lacking the friendship of human beings, keep in mind that when we give ourselves to others they will often give themselves to us.

> *Father, whatever the reason for my loneliness, help me take these words to heart. Drive the truth deeply into my spirit that I need to be a friend. In Jesus' name, Amen.*

WHEN LONELINESS PREVAILS

WHEN FORGIVING IS NOT EASY ⸺

—Consider the extent of divine forgiveness.
As far as the east is from the west,
    so far has he removed our transgressions from us. (Ps. 103:12)

—God—the only Avenger of evil.
Do not take revenge, my friends, but leave room for God's wrath, for it is written: "It is mine to avenge; I will repay," says the Lord. (Rom. 12:19)

—What God has done for us we must do for others.
Bear with each other and forgive whatever grievances you may have against one another. Forgive as the Lord forgave you. (Col. 3:13)

—Unforgiveness ruins our lives.
See to it that no one misses the grace of God and that no bitter root grows up to cause trouble and defile many. (Heb. 12:15)

—Forgiveness—the main message of Christianity.
That God was reconciling the world to himself in Christ, not counting men's sins against them. And he has committed to us the message of reconciliation. (2 Cor. 5:19)

—Satan is unable to get a foothold among the forgiving.
If you forgive anyone, I also forgive him. And what I have forgiven . . . I have forgiven in the sight of Christ for your sake, in order that Satan might not outwit us. For we are not unaware of his schemes. (2 Cor. 2:10–11)

—Our refusal to forgive others impedes God's forgiveness of us.
And when you stand praying, if you hold anything against anyone, forgive him, so that your Father in heaven may forgive you your sins. (Mark 11:25)

—Serious consequences follow when we refuse to forgive.
This is how my heavenly Father will treat each of you unless you forgive your brother from your heart. (Matt. 18:35)

7

Some think Christianity sets an impossible standard when it calls on believers to forgive all those who have hurt or injured them. But with God "all things are possible." There are three main reasons why we may find it difficult to forgive.

First, we do not have a sufficiently deep realization of how much we ourselves have been forgiven. The sin of another against us is as nothing when compared to our sin against God—yet he has forgiven us.

Second, holding resentment or indignation against another who has hurt us gives us a sense of power and control over them, and when we give it up, we are left feeling somewhat helpless. But it is to helplessness we are called in the words: "'It is mine to avenge; I will repay,' says the Lord" (Rom. 12:19). Forgiveness involves giving up control and trusting God with the outcome.

A third reason why we may find it hard to forgive is what we might call "misplaced dependency." This occurs when we erroneously believe that another person's positive interaction with us is essential to our feeling good about ourselves, and so we move from dependency on God to dependency on others. Then when they hurt us, *because we believe we need them to function*, we feel they have destroyed our souls. This is why we are always hurt most by those who are closest to us. But people cannot destroy us; only God can do that (Matt. 10:28). It is a lot easier to forgive when we see that our life is not in people, but in God.

Forgiveness, we must remember, is not so much a feeling but a decision—an action of the will. You *decide* to forgive, whether you feel like it or not. You supply the willingness, God will supply the power.

> O Father, give me a deeper realization than ever before
> of how much I have been forgiven. And forgive me
> again for preferring control over trust and for finding my
> life in people rather than in you. You have forgiven me.
> Help me to forgive others. In Jesus' name, Amen.

WHEN YOU LAPSE INTO SELF-PITY ———

—We are prone to depend on sources other than God.
Woe to those who go down to Egypt for help,
    who rely on horses,
who trust in the multitude of their chariots
    and in the great strength of their horsemen,
but do not look to the Holy One of Israel, or seek help from the
    LORD. (Isa. 31:1)

—God alone is the source of our strength.
Have mercy on me, O God, have mercy on me,
    for in you my soul takes refuge.
I will take refuge in the shadow of your wings
    until the disaster has passed. (Ps. 57:1)

—The divine invitation to trust.
Cast all your anxiety on him because he cares for you. (1 Pet. 5:7)

—A decision all must make.
Trust in the LORD with all your heart
    and lean not on your own understanding. (Prov. 3:5)

—Blessing comes from trust.
Blessed is the man
    who makes the LORD his trust. (Ps. 40:4)

—Where there is no repentance, there is spiritual death.
Godly sorrow brings repentance that leads to salvation and leaves no
regret, but worldly sorrow brings death. (2 Cor. 7:10)

—The way to repent.
Grieve, mourn and wail. Change your laughter to mourning and your
joy to gloom. Humble yourselves before the Lord, and he will lift you
up. (James 4:9–10)

—Maintain other-centeredness.
Each of you should look not only to your own interests, but also to
the interests of others. (Phil. 2:4)

8

One of the greatest dangers that can befall us when we find ourselves overtaken by sorrow is to lapse into self-pity. Yet it is easy to do this. Self-pity is the "Poor Me Syndrome"; it is pouring pity on ourselves in the hope that the pain we are experiencing may be assuaged.

Sensitive people are most prone to self-pity because they are easily hurt. Sensitivity is a capacity for sympathy and is God's equipment to help us feel deeply with others. Used in this way it is a wonderful thing. When it causes us to turn inwards on ourselves, however, it is a violation of God's design for us and drags us down into the most miserable of moods.

The real problem with self-pity is that it replaces God in our lives by a self-centered attempt to deal with our pain. Instead of turning to God in the midst of our difficulties and bringing our pain to him, we prefer the temporary anodyne of self-pity. We cringe, we whine, we sigh, we complain, we accuse God of forgetting to be gracious; and in this self-engrossed frame of mind we regard our small personal problems as more serious than some of the major tragedies in the lives of others. The pity we lavish upon ourselves eases the pain, but it does so in a way that ignores God.

Self-pity is sensitiveness turned to selfishness; we prefer our own way of dealing with our pain to God's way. The only real remedy for self-pity is repentance. We must repent of our stubborn commitment to independently dealing with life's problems and assuaging our pain instead of turning in helpless abandonment to God. Then and only then can self-pity be expelled.

> O God, forgive me that I prefer drawing on my own resources rather than yours whenever I am in personal pain. I repent of this deeply ingrained tendency within me and turn to you for comfort, healing, and release. In Jesus' name, Amen.

WHEN YOU LAPSE INTO SELF-PITY ———

—Advice concerning wrong comparisons.
We do not dare to classify or compare ourselves with some who commend themselves. When they measure themselves by themselves and compare themselves with themselves, they are not wise. . . . For it is not the one who commends himself who is approved, but the one whom the Lord commends. (2 Cor. 10:12, 18)

—Continued jealousy—a mark of immaturity and worldliness.
You are still worldly. For since there is jealousy and quarreling among you, are you not worldly? Are you not acting like mere men? (1 Cor. 3:3)

—Love—the only answer to jealousy.
Love is patient, love is kind. It does not envy, it does not boast, it is not proud. (1 Cor. 13:4)

—We must compare ourselves constantly with Christ.
Let us fix our eyes on Jesus, the author and perfecter of our faith, who for the joy set before him endured the cross, scorning its shame, and sat down at the right hand of the throne of God. (Heb. 12:2)

—Jealousy upsets the physical system.
A heart at peace gives life to the body,
    but envy rots the bones. (Prov. 14:30)

—A decision all Christians must make.
Therefore, rid yourselves of all malice and all deceit, hypocrisy, envy, and slander of every kind. (1 Pet. 2:1)

—Jealousy dies in a heart where Christ truly lives.
This is how we know what love is: Jesus Christ laid down his life for us. And we ought to lay down our lives for our brothers. (1 John 3:16)

—Fix your eyes only on the Lord.
My eyes are ever on the LORD, for only he will release my feet from the snare. (Ps. 25:15)

9

The word *jealousy* is used in two different ways in Scripture, and this fact must always be borne in mind. There is a good jealousy and a bad jealousy. God describes himself on one occasion as "jealous" (Exod. 20:5), and Paul said to the Corinthians: "I am jealous for you with a godly jealousy" (2 Cor. 11:2). These are expressions of a good jealousy—a passion and zeal for the one loved, not for one's own interests or concerns.

The word *jealousy*, however, is rarely used in this sense in today's world. When we speak of jealousy in ordinary conversation we usually refer not to good jealousy but to bad jealousy. Bad jealousy is the feeling of coldness and resentment we experience when others against whom we match ourselves in thought, appearance, or accomplishment are singled out for praise or commendation. Jealousy is not normally directed against those who are far above us in attainment; usually it is focused on those in our immediate circle, on those whom we regard as being on a par with ourselves or inferior to ourselves. A Latin proverb puts it this way: "The potter is envious of the potter, the smith of the smith." *Jealousy is rooted in a wrong comparison with others.* "It is envy born of some deep love of self," said one preacher.

The practice of comparing ourselves with others can swiftly lead to sin. If we feel another is not as good as we are, we can fall prey to pride; if we feel he or she is better than we, we are tempted to imply they are hypocrites; if they are more successful than we, we often slide into envy.

Jealousy can be dealt with only by keeping our eyes firmly fixed on Jesus and satisfying the impulse for comparison by comparing ourselves with him alone.

> *O God, forgive me for my mistaken acts of comparison—comparing myself with others when I ought to be comparing myself with your Son. May I be so taken up with him and so secure in him that I can look at others with love, not envy. In Christ's name I pray, Amen.*

WHEN JEALOUS THOUGHTS INVADE ——

~

WHEN PRAYING NO LONGER APPEALS —

—Prayer is more than a suggestion—it is a command.
Then Jesus told his disciples a parable to show them that they should always pray and not give up. (Luke 18:1)

—Prayer is to be perpetual, not merely occasional.
Look to the Lord and his strength; seek his face always. (Ps. 105:4)

—Asking and receiving give impetus and joy to prayer.
Until now you have not asked for anything in my name. Ask and you will receive, and your joy will be complete. (John 16:24)

—Prayer is to be offered at all times.
And pray in the Spirit on all occasions with all kinds of prayers and requests. With this in mind, be alert and always keep on praying for all the saints. (Eph. 6:18)

—It is the first thing we ought to do when in trouble.
Is any one of you in trouble? He should pray. (James 5:13)

—Prayer is to be offered for all people.
I urge, then, first of all, that requests, prayers, intercession and thanksgiving be made for everyone. (1 Tim. 2:1)

—Hope dies when we lose contact with God.
Why are you downcast, O my soul?
    Why so disturbed within me?
Put your hope in God,
    for I will yet praise him,
        my Savior and my God. (Ps. 42:5)

—An example to follow.
I cry aloud to the LORD;
    I lift up my voice to the LORD for mercy.
I pour out my complaint before him;
    before him I tell my trouble. (Ps. 142:1–2)

10

The obstacles to prayer are many. Some claim they don't have *time* to pray, yet they can easily find time for other things: the newspaper, television, leisure activities, and so on. Christ, you remember, stole time from sleep to pray. Others who live in crowded accommodations claim they have no *place* to pray. Well, it's always possible to go for a walk with Jesus. What conversation one can have with the Lord on a long walk! Still others complain they don't know *what* to pray for. Then make a list—friends and loved ones who need to be converted, those known to you who are sick, the needs of the church you attend, your own needs, and so on.

By far the most common obstacle to prayer, however, is *disinclination*. People do not pray because they do not feel like it. But we must not assume that prayer is effective only when it arises from an eager and emotional heart. Those who have achieved great power in prayer tell us that floods of feeling come only now and again in their times of intercession. They say we must learn to keep our appointments with God *whether we feel like it or not*. If we have an appointment to meet someone whom we regard as important, do we break it a few moments before the meeting because we feel disinclined? Common courtesy tells us it would not be right. Are we to be less courteous with God?

The great practitioners of prayer assure us God can do more with us when we pray against our inclination than when we pray with it. The willingness to submit to him deepens our surrender; our resolve to go to God builds steel into our Christian commitment. It is faith, not feeling, that measures the efficacy of prayer.

> O God, I see how fickle I have been in allowing obstacles to override my commitment and dedication. Forgive me for this. I make a fresh commitment now and pray for strength to overcome everything, including the problem of disinclination. In Jesus' name, Amen.

WHEN PRAYING NO LONGER APPEALS —

WHEN DOUBTS ASSAIL ───────────

—A man who brought his doubt to Jesus.
"'If you can'?" said Jesus. "Everything is possible for him who believes." Immediately the boy's father exclaimed, "I do believe; help me overcome my unbelief!" (Mark 9:23–24)

—How Christ accommodated Thomas's doubts.
Then he said to Thomas, "Put your finger here; see my hands. Reach out your hand and put it into my side. Stop doubting and believe." Thomas said to him, "My Lord and my God!" Then Jesus told him, "Because you have seen me, you have believed; blessed are those who have not seen and yet have believed." (John 20:27–29)

—A talk with God can turn doubt to discovery.
Then Job replied to the LORD: "I know that you can do all things;
    no plan of yours can be thwarted . . .
You said, 'Listen now, and I will speak;
    I will question you,
    and you shall answer me.'
My ears had heard of you
    but now my eyes have seen you." (Job 42:1–2, 4–5)

—Doubt when undealt with produces a turbulent spirit.
But when he asks, he must believe and not doubt, because he who doubts is like a wave of the sea, blown and tossed by the wind. (James 1:6)

—Perusing Scripture—the chief remedy for doubt.
Consequently, faith comes from hearing the message, and the message is heard through the word of Christ. (Rom. 10:17)

—Doubt robs faith.
Jesus replied, "I tell you the truth, if you have faith and do not doubt, not only can you do what was done to the fig tree, but also you can say to this mountain, 'Go, throw yourself into the sea,' and it will be done." (Matt. 21:21)

—Doubt dies when one sees this truth.
Jesus Christ is the same yesterday and today and forever. (Heb. 13:8)

11

Many Christians feel that if doubt exists in their minds they cannot be true believers. This arises from a wrong understanding of the nature of doubt. "Doubt," said Os Guinness, "is a state of mind in suspension between faith and unbelief so that it is neither of them wholly, and it is each only partly. *It is faith in two minds.*" Every Christian must understand this, for it gives the lie to the idea that when a believer doubts, he or she betrays the faith and surrenders to unbelief. No misunderstanding causes more havoc and spiritual damage to Christians than this.

Perhaps we can better understand doubt by taking the analogy of fear. Many think fear is the opposite of courage, but it is not. The opposite of fear is cowardice. Fear is the halfway stage between the two. It is not wrong to feel fear in certain situations. The real question is what do we do with it—something courageous or something cowardly? It is the same with doubt. It stands undecided between faith and unbelief and has to choose between the two. The presence of doubt is not the problem; the critical issue is what we do with it when it arises.

A man one day came to Jesus and confessed to his struggle with doubt (Mark 9:14–29). The struggle with doubt must be seen as a sign of faith, not unbelief. What destroys faith is not doubt but disobedience—the unwillingness to bring those doubts and lay them at the feet of Jesus. The prayer of the man described in Mark 9—"I do believe; help me overcome my unbelief!"—is one that all of us must echo whenever we are caught in the throes of doubt. This attitude changes everything. "I believe, but I want to believe even more."

> *Father, thank you for reminding me that doubt is not*
> *the opposite of faith, but faith in two minds. I bring all*
> *my doubts now to you and confess that I believe. Yet I*
> *want to believe more. Help me, dear Father. In Jesus'*
> *name, Amen.*

WHEN DOUBTS ASSAIL

WHEN YOU FACE FAILURE ─────────

—God knows your situation and feels for you in your pain.
O LORD, you have searched me and you know me. You know when I sit and when I rise; you perceive my thoughts from afar. You discern my going out and my lying down; you are familiar with all my ways. (Ps. 139:1–3)

—A promise to hold on to.
If the LORD delights in a man's way, he makes his steps firm; though he stumble, he will not fall, for the LORD upholds him with his hand. (Ps. 37:23–24)

—God's attention never wavers.
For the eyes of the LORD range throughout the earth to strengthen those whose hearts are fully committed to him. (2 Chron. 16:9)

—Use discouraging situations to draw closer to God.
One thing I ask of the LORD, this is what I seek: that I may dwell in the house of the LORD all the days of my life, to gaze upon the beauty of the LORD and to seek him in his temple. (Ps. 27:4)

—Consider the power that is at your disposal.
And his incomparably great power for us who believe. That power is like the working of his mighty strength, which he exerted in Christ when he raised him from the dead and seated him at his right hand in the heavenly realms. (Eph. 1:19–20)

—Focus on finding God's purposes for your life.
If any of you lacks wisdom, he should ask God, who gives generously to all without finding fault, and it will be given to him. (James 1:5)

—God promises help and guidance for a better future.
My son, do not forget my teaching, but keep my commands in your heart, for they will prolong your life many years and bring you prosperity. (Prov. 3:1–2)

12

It's hard to look objectively at things when one has failed. When Millais first exhibited his *Ophelia* in 1852, one critic dubbed it "O Failure!" It is said that Millais was plagued by these words for the rest of his life.

When you are overtaken by failure, sit down as soon as possible and prayerfully begin to analyze the reason for the failure. Consider the possibility that God may have allowed this failure because it was part of his purpose for your life. Many have discovered that God allowed failure in their lives to turn their thoughts in a new direction of service for him.

If, however, *after prayer* and careful consideration of this possibility you are sure you have God's approval for continuing along the same lines, then ask yourself: Have I contributed to this failure by my inattention to detail, lack of preparation, naïveté, wrong timing, failure to weigh the pros and cons, disregard of moral principles, insensitivity to other people's feelings, and so on? Having learned the lessons that come from failure, try again.

A Christian poster I once saw in a bookshop showed the picture of a man with his arms folded and a look of resignation on his face. Printed on his T-shirt was the admission "I gave up." In the corner of the poster, barely visible, was a drawing of a little black hill and on it a very tiny cross. These words were printed beneath it: "*I didn't.*" The One who triumphed over all obstacles holds out his hands to you. Take his hand, and if another purpose has not been shown you, try again.

> *Father, I see that no failure is a failure if it succeeds in driving me to your side. Show me your will and purposes for my life, and if it be that I should try again, then help me do it in your strength and not in my own. In Christ's name I pray, Amen.*

WHEN YOU FACE FAILURE

—God's throne will never be overturned.
But about the Son he says, "Your throne, O God, will last for ever and ever, and righteousness will be the scepter of your kingdom." (Heb. 1:8)

—The anchor of hope.
We have this hope as an anchor for the soul, firm and secure. It enters the inner sanctuary behind the curtain. (Heb. 6:19)

—God's "Yes" makes all the difference.
For no matter how many promises God has made, they are "Yes" in Christ. And so through him the "Amen" is spoken by us to the glory of God. (2 Cor. 1:20)

—The One who remains sure and steadfast.
The Maker of heaven and earth,
    the sea, and everything in them—
    the LORD, who remains faithful forever. (Ps. 146:6)

—God's covenants cannot be broken.
Know therefore that the LORD your God is God; he is the faithful God, keeping his covenant of love to a thousand generations of those who love him and keep his commands. (Deut. 7:9)

—Wait and see what the Lord will do.
Yet the LORD longs to be gracious to you; he rises to show you compassion. For the LORD is a God of justice. Blessed are all who wait for him! (Isa. 30:18)

—When divine waiting turns to divine acting.
I the LORD have spoken. The time has come for me to act. I will not hold back. (Ezek. 24:14)

—It's impossible for God to lie.
Because God wanted to make the unchanging nature of his purpose very clear to the heirs of what was promised, he confirmed it with an oath. God did this so that, by two unchangeable things in which it is impossible for God to lie, we who have fled to take hold of the hope offered to us may be greatly encouraged. (Heb. 6:17–18)

13

Hope is one of the cardinal values of the Christian faith. "These three remain," said the apostle Paul in 1 Corinthians 13:13, "faith, hope and love." All through the New Testament, hope is spoken of in the highest terms. It's sad, therefore, when a quality given such prominence in Scripture is missing in human life.

We must differentiate, however, between the word *hope* as it is used in Scripture and the way it is used in ordinary conversation. We sometimes hear people say, "I hope things will get better" or "I am hoping for an increase in my salary," but we are not given any guarantees in Scripture that everything we "hope" for in this sense will come our way. When the Bible talks about hope it is talking about the certainty we have as Christians that *God's eternal purposes will never be thwarted and that all his promises will come to pass.* And clinging to that fact enables us to face and handle all those times in life when earthly hopes and ambitions are dashed.

The thing that gives a Christian what the writer to the Hebrews calls a hope "both sure and steadfast" (Heb. 6:19 KJV) is the fact that *God is on the throne.* Have you noticed in the Scriptures that whenever God's servants were in trouble they were given a vision of the eternal throne? Isaiah . . . David . . . Ezekiel . . . the apostle John. Why a throne? Because God *rules* from his throne, and no matter if appearances are to the contrary, he is always in control. The hope (or certainty) that God's purposes continue even if ours get pushed aside acts as an anchor to the soul. We must never forget it.

> *Loving Father and Most Holy God, let the hope that is "both sure and steadfast" hold me safe and secure, particularly in those times when my personal hopes are not realized. All things proceed according to your will. May I ever rejoice in that, Amen.*

WHEN HOPES ARE DASHED

WHEN ONE THING COMES AFTER ———
ANOTHER

—The first thing to do when you're in trouble.
I want men everywhere to lift up holy hands in prayer, without anger or disputing. (1 Tim. 2:8)

—Understand the purpose behind all trials.
Consider it pure joy, my brothers, whenever you face trials of many kinds, because you know that the testing of your faith develops perseverance. Perseverance must finish its work so that you may be mature and complete, not lacking anything. (James 1:2–4)

—Cling closely to God.
Have mercy on me, O God, have mercy on me, for in you my soul takes refuge. I will take refuge in the shadow of your wings until the disaster has passed. (Ps. 57:1)

—God always brings us through.
The righteous cry out, and the LORD hears them;
he delivers them from all their troubles. (Ps. 34:17)

—Why we should never lose confidence in God.
Though you have made me see troubles, many and bitter, you will restore my life again; from the depths of the earth you will again bring me up. (Ps. 71:20)

—Remind yourself of past divine deliverances.
I will remember the deeds of the LORD;
    yes, I will remember your miracles of long ago.
I will meditate on all your works
    and consider all your mighty deeds. (Ps. 77:11–12)

—A promise that will never be broken.
The LORD is close to the brokenhearted
    and saves those who are crushed in spirit. (Ps. 34:18)

—Everything else may fail—but God? Never.
God is our refuge and strength, an ever-present help in trouble. Therefore we will not fear, though the earth give way and the mountains fall into the heart of the sea. (Ps. 46:1–2)

14

"When sorrows come, they come not in single spies but in battalions," said Shakespeare in *Hamlet*. We have all noticed it too. Troubles have an uncanny way of coming together. For a while everything goes along pleasantly, and then suddenly the whole world tumbles around our ears. Nobody fully understands why it is that troubles seem to arrive in swarms. Many have tried to explain this strange rhythmic law, but when all has been said it still remains a mystery.

What is not a mystery, though, is that God never withdraws from us no matter how many troubles we face. It was Emerson who said: "Bad times have a *scientific* value. They are occasions a good learner would not miss." But most of us are not "good" learners. We much prefer a carefree life to mastering the lessons that accompany the shadowed way. A lesson we must learn, however, is that in times of difficulty and stress *we come to a fresh and vivid realization of our dependency on God*. When things are going well we have confidence in our ability to look after our own affairs. We feel we are able to handle things *alone*. But when difficulties crowd in upon us and hedge us on every side then our confidence evaporates; we are reminded in a dramatic way of our frailty, and we cry out to the Lord for his help. At such times we begin to realize we are not so strong and self-sufficient as we thought we were.

That discovery is worth making. It produces in us a humility that compels us to lift up praying hands to the Lord. We learn best the meaning of dependency on God not on the starlit way but on the shadowed way.

> Gracious God, when will I learn that the Christian life is not my responsibility, but my response to your ability? Help me throw myself on you and begin to learn in a new way the great art of dependency. In Jesus' name, Amen.

WHEN ONE THING COMES AFTER ——— ANOTHER

WHEN CRIPPLED BY FEELINGS———
OF INFERIORITY

—Made in God's image—His highest compliment.
So God created man in his own image,
    in the image of God he created him;
    male and female he created them. (Gen. 1:27)

—God sees what others can't.
The LORD does not look at the things man looks at. Man looks at the outward appearance, but the LORD looks at the heart. (1 Sam. 16:7)

—The danger of wrong comparisons.
Each one should test his own actions. Then he can take pride in himself, without comparing himself to somebody else. (Gal. 6:4)

—Be balanced in your estimate of yourself.
For by the grace given me I say to every one of you: Do not think of yourself more highly than you ought, but rather think of yourself with sober judgment, in accordance with the measure of faith God has given you. (Rom. 12:3)

—Self-condemnation contradicts the divine edict.
Therefore, there is now no condemnation for those who are in Christ Jesus. (Rom. 8:1)

—You are the work of God's hands.
For we are God's workmanship, created in Christ Jesus to do good works, which God prepared in advance for us to do. (Eph. 2:10)

—Heirs of God ought not to think of themselves as inferior.
So you are no longer a slave, but a son; and since you are a son, God has made you also an heir. (Gal. 4:7)

—You are part of an eternal purpose.
And we, who with unveiled faces all reflect the Lord's glory, are being transformed into his likeness with ever-increasing glory, which comes from the Lord, who is the Spirit. (2 Cor. 3:18)

15

Frequently in these modern times one hears the term *inferiority complex* bandied about. It describes the low sense of self-worth some people carry around with them, the consequence usually of ineffective parenting. Parents—even good parents—can sometimes give their children the idea that they love them *for* something: if they work hard, if they come up to their expectations, if they are very clever. Children then come to see their worth based on how well they perform rather than who they are. A low sense of worth may blight a whole life and, at its worst, can develop into self-rejection, even hate. Most people learn how to cope with the problem by keeping away from situations in which they might be shown up as inferior, and thus live their lives at a lower level than God intends.

Whatever forces have gone into shaping our thoughts and ideas about ourselves (and we must be careful not to hold bitterness or resentment against those who nurtured us), we who are Christians must stand before God and draw the estimate of ourselves from him. However little worth there may be in our nature, Jesus put worth upon us by dying for our salvation. No one is to be despised (not even by himself or herself) when they were dear enough to Christ that he shed his sacred blood. That is the ground of our worth—the solid, sufficient, and only basis for it. *And it is the same for everyone.*

This last statement must be allowed to soak into our minds, for it is only when we see that worth is not something that is earned but something *bestowed* that self-despising can be rooted out of our minds.

> O Father, help me see myself as you see me—a child of
> God and a joint heir with Christ. Your Son displayed
> no inferiority, and now that I am in him, neither ought
> I. Bring my thinking in line with your thinking, dear
> Father. In Christ's name I pray, Amen.

WHEN CRIPPLED BY FEELINGS
OF INFERIORITY

WHEN YOU WONDER IF GOD CAN TRANSFORM THINGS

—The work at which God excels.
And we know that in all things God works for the good of those who love him, who have been called according to his purpose. (Rom. 8:28)

—If God can do this he can do anything.
God has raised this Jesus to life, and we are all witnesses of the fact. (Acts 2:32)

—The power through which transformation comes.
But by the grace of God I am what I am, and his grace to me was not without effect. No, I worked harder than all of them—yet not I, but the grace of God that was with me. (1 Cor. 15:10)

—In God's time.
He has made everything beautiful in its time. He has also set eternity in the hearts of men; yet they cannot fathom what God has done from beginning to end. (Eccles. 3:11)

—Truth will always prevail.
For we cannot do anything against the truth, but only for the truth. (2 Cor. 13:8)

—Take confidence in this.
Now to him who is able to do immeasurably more than all we ask or imagine, according to his power that is at work within us. (Eph. 3:20)

—Men's intentions are overruled by God's intentions.
"You intended to harm me, but God intended it for good to accomplish what is now being done, the saving of many lives." (Gen. 50:20)

—The final great act of transformation.
Then I saw a new heaven and a new earth, for the first heaven and the first earth had passed away, and there was no longer any sea. (Rev. 21:1)

16

Can God really take the awful situations that befall us, as well as the calamities we bring on ourselves by our own foolishness, and turn them to good? The Bible says he can: "And we know that in all things God works for the good of those who love him, who have been called according to his purpose" (Rom. 8:28). Yet some still struggle to believe it.

The best way to deepen the conviction that God really can take the setbacks of life and turn them into springboards is to think of the Cross. That is the supreme example of God's ability to transform things. There he took the foulest event that ever happened on this earth and made it into the most sublime. The crucifixion was the world's worst crime; now it is the world's supreme hope. It was the darkest scene in human history; now it is the brightest. If we had a close friend who was executed we wouldn't be inclined to walk around with a small replica of a gallows or an electric chair around our necks. But the manner of Christ's dying—the Cross—we parade in every way we can: the top of church steeples is not too high for it; the communion table barely prominent enough. A line from one of our Christian hymns puts it like this: "He hung and suffered *there*." The Cross now bears God's message, not the message of men. They gave out hate; he gave back love. Sin became the dark backdrop against which his grace shines more brilliantly.

If God can do that with the Cross, what might he not do with the evil that strikes into our lives? If such a dark deed as the crucifixion was not beyond his power to transform, will he be beaten by the evil things that afflict our lives? The answer must be no.

> *Father, help me drop my anchor into the depths of this reassuring and encouraging revelation: that nothing that ever happens to me is beyond your power to transform. Every stumbling block becomes a stepping-stone. I am so grateful, Amen.*

WHEN YOU WONDER IF GOD
CAN TRANSFORM THINGS

WHEN YOU FALL INTO ———————
GRIEVOUS SIN

—The first thing to do when overtaken by sin.
If we confess our sins, he is faithful and just and will forgive us our sins and purify us from all unrighteousness. (1 John 1:9)

—How to guard against the entry of further sin.
Rather, clothe yourselves with the Lord Jesus Christ, and do not think about how to gratify the desires of the sinful nature. (Rom. 13:14)

—The joy of forgiveness.
Blessed is he whose transgressions are forgiven, whose sins are covered. Blessed is the man whose sin the LORD does not count against him and in whose spirit is no deceit. (Ps. 32:1–2)

—A sinner's prayer.
Have mercy on me, O God, according to your unfailing love; according to your great compassion blot out my transgressions. Wash away all my iniquity and cleanse me from my sin. (Ps. 51:1–2)

—Remind yourself constantly of this.
You are forgiving and good, O Lord,
    abounding in love to all who call to you. (Ps. 86:5)

—Why God should be reverenced.
But with you there is forgiveness;
    therefore you are feared. (Ps. 130:4)

—The extent of divine forgiveness.
As far as the east is from the west,
    so far has he removed our transgressions from us. (Ps. 103:12)

—The dynamics of true repentance.
Come near to God and he will come near to you. Wash your hands, you sinners, and purify your hearts, you double-minded. Grieve, mourn and wail. Change your laughter to mourning and your joy to gloom. Humble yourselves before the Lord, and he will lift you up. (James 4:8–10)

17

It is sad when a Christian falls into sin, but it is not the end. Whether others know about it or not, *God knows*, and that is why the matter must be dealt with first before him. Sin, it has been said, is not so much the breaking of God's laws as the breaking of his heart. How then do we relieve the hurt that lies upon the heart of God when we have fallen into grievous sin?

First, we must not minimize the sin. Nowadays there is a tendency to use euphemistic language to describe sin. If a moral mishap has occurred we say it was just a "little" thing or "it wasn't important." Cancer in the stomach is still cancer even though a person may pass off the discomfort as "a bit of indigestion." A lie is *more* than a fib. Stealing is *more* than scrounging. Adultery is *more* than an extramarital relationship. We don't make a deadly thing innocuous by giving it a different name.

Second, we must confess the sin to God. We must cry out to him as did the psalmist: "Have mercy on me, O God, / according to your unfailing love . . . blot out my transgressions. / Wash away all my iniquity / and cleanse me from my sin" (Ps. 51:1–2).

Third, if the sin has involved others, then we must seek to put things right with them also. It is always helpful to discuss this matter with a minister or a Christian counselor, however, before embarking on a course of action so as to avoid unnecessary complications.

Fourth, we must walk into the future clean and more dependent than ever on God's empowering grace. All the resources of heaven are engaged against sin, and the reason why we fall into it is because we do not avail ourselves of those resources.

> *Gracious and forgiving God, I do not minimize my sin or argue against its enormity, but I bring it now to you for your forgiveness: I repent and receive the pardon you so graciously offer me in Christ. Thank you, my Father, Amen.*

WHEN YOU FALL INTO ———
GRIEVOUS SIN

WHEN OVERCOME BY SHAME

—The look that saved.
The Lord turned and looked straight at Peter. Then Peter remembered the word the Lord had spoken to him: "Before the rooster crows today, you will disown me three times." And he went outside and wept bitterly. (Luke 22:61–62)

—The Christian hope knows no shame.
No one whose hope is in you
    will ever be put to shame,
but they will be put to shame
    who are treacherous without excuse. (Ps. 25:3)

—How to avoid shame in the future.
Oh, that my ways were steadfast
    in obeying your decrees!
Then I would not be put to shame
    when I consider all your commands. (Ps. 119:5–6)

—God can do more than forgive.
If we confess our sins, he is faithful and just and will forgive us our sins and purify us from all unrighteousness. (1 John 1:9)

—Concealed sins are unforgiven sins.
He who conceals his sins does not prosper,
    but whoever confesses and renounces them finds mercy. (Prov. 28:13)

—Take heart from this.
Who is a God like you,
    who pardons sin and forgives the transgression
    of the remnant of his inheritance?
You do not stay angry forever
    but delight to show mercy. (Mic. 7:18)

—What intimacy with God involves.
Let us draw near to God with a sincere heart in full assurance of faith, having our hearts sprinkled to cleanse us from a guilty conscience and having our bodies washed with pure water. (Heb. 10:22)

18

The worst state into which any man or woman can fall is to be without shame. Sin is always deadly, but never more deadly than when it cannot be shamed. We never see the anger of Jesus in the New Testament more fierce than when it blazed against those who, because they lacked shame, seemed insulated against correction—the Pharisees, for example.

Shame consists of several strands: fear of exposure, abhorrence at the discovery of one's deficiency, and dread of the consequences. Before they sinned Adam and Eve were "naked, and . . . felt no shame" (Gen. 2:25), but afterwards the shame of what they had done led them to cover their nakedness with fig leaves. They were so fearful of being exposed that, when God came down, they hid among the trees. They did not want to be *seen*.

Shame abhors not only exposure but the discovery of some inner deficiency, which in turn leads to self-consciousness and self-hate. We feel angry with ourselves that we could have behaved in such a way: "Fancy me doing *that!*"

Shame dreads consequences also, the anticipated outcome of being found out. It could mean rejection by others, the making of restitution, the facing of unpleasant situations.

But grave though shame is, it is not beyond the redeeming power of Jesus. When we bring before him the matter that caused the shame, he is swift to forgive and to restore our sense of dignity. In a sense we can be grateful for shame. It is a blessing in disguise. Without it we might continue on a downward course without being aware of the degradation that is going on in our soul. If there is one thing worse than shame, it is to be unashamed.

> *Gracious and loving God, I bring this deep sense of*
> *shame that is upon me and offer it to you. Help me*
> *identify the cause of it and deal with it now in your*
> *mighty name. Cleanse me and set me free. In Jesus'*
> *name, Amen.*

WHEN OVERCOME BY SHAME ———

WHEN LAID OFF
OR UNEMPLOYED

—*Christ knows and feels every one of our hurts.*
For we do not have a high priest who is unable to sympathize with our weaknesses, but we have one who has been tempted in every way, just as we are—yet was without sin. Let us then approach the throne of grace with confidence, so that we may receive mercy and find grace to help us in our time of need. (Heb. 4:15–16)

—*Grace flows in to meet every need.*
But he said to me, "My grace is sufficient for you, for my power is made perfect in weakness." Therefore I will boast all the more gladly about my weaknesses, so that Christ's power may rest on me. (2 Cor. 12:9)

—*Worth is not something earned but something bestowed.*
He predestined us to be adopted as his sons through Jesus Christ, in accordance with his pleasure and will—to the praise of his glorious grace, which he has freely given us in the One he loves. (Eph. 1:5–6)

—*An eternal purpose is at work in us.*
And we, who with unveiled faces all reflect the Lord's glory, are being transformed into his likeness with ever-increasing glory, which comes from the Lord, who is the Spirit. (2 Cor. 3:18)

—*Understand what being a child of God means.*
Now if we are children, then we are heirs—heirs of God and co-heirs with Christ, if indeed we share in his sufferings in order that we may also share in his glory. (Rom. 8:17)

—*Our identity is only complete in Christ.*
And you have been given fullness in Christ, who is the head over every power and authority. (Col. 2:10)

—*There is no redundancy or unemployment in the church of God.*
Now you are the body of Christ, and each one of you is a part of it. (1 Cor. 12:27)

19

Nothing can plunge the soul into a depressed or disconsolate mood more effectively than when one is laid off or is unemployed. At such times one feels frustrated, devalued, worthless, and insignificant. The intensity of these feelings will vary, however, depending on whether we draw our sense of worth from what we do or from who we are. If we draw our feelings of worth from the things we do (our job, profession, performance, etc.) then when our circumstances prevent us from contributing as we have done, the usual emotional response is to feel shattered. Those who draw their sense of worth from who they are recognize that, although they can no longer contribute (either temporarily or permanently), their worth as a person remains intact, and they will have a quite different emotional response. They will feel shaken but not shattered.

The way our emotions react is directly related to the way we perceive and evaluate what has happened to us. This is why one of the most crucial issues to settle in life is the understanding of where our worth truly lies—is it in who we are or in what we do? What we do in our work is important but not all-important. The most important thing in life, *and the balancing factor in all of life's problems,* is to know exactly who we are and where our true worth lies. As Christians our worth lies in the fact that we belong to God, that we are heirs of God and joint heirs with Christ (Rom. 8:17). Taking hold of this truth will not stop us from hurting when life becomes difficult, but it can mean the difference between being shaken or being shattered.

> *Father, I am grateful for all the skills you have given me, but I see they are not everything. You are everything. Help me from now on to draw my worth primarily from you rather than from what I do. In Jesus' name I pray, Amen.*

WHEN LAID OFF
OR UNEMPLOYED

WHEN IT'S DIFFICULT TO ─────── BE GENEROUS

—The peril faced by the ungenerous.
If a man shuts his ears to the cry of the poor,
    he too will cry out and not be answered. (Prov. 21:13)

—Prosperity lies in giving, not getting.
A generous man will prosper;
    he who refreshes others will himself be refreshed. (Prov. 11:25)

—The reward of the generous.
And if anyone gives even a cup of cold water to one of these little ones because he is my disciple, I tell you the truth, he will certainly not lose his reward. (Matt. 10:42)

—Putting God first and before others.
Honor the LORD with your wealth,
    with the firstfruits of all your crops;
then your barns will be filled to overflowing,
    and your vats will brim over with new wine. (Prov. 3:9–10)

—It's not only what you give but how you give that matters.
Give generously to him and do so without a grudging heart; then because of this the LORD your God will bless you in all your work and in everything you put your hand to. (Deut. 15:10)

—The measure of your giving is the measure of your receiving.
"Give, and it will be given to you. A good measure, pressed down, shaken together and running over, will be poured into your lap. For with the measure you use, it will be measured to you." (Luke 6:38)

—Grace abounds where generosity abounds.
Remember this: Whoever sows sparingly will also reap sparingly, and whoever sows generously will also reap generously. Each man should give what he has decided in his heart to give, not reluctantly or under compulsion, for God loves a cheerful giver. And God is able to make all grace abound to you, so that in all things at all times, having all that you need, you will abound in every good work. (2 Cor. 9:6–8)

20

Perhaps nothing is as revealing of our dedication to Christ and his cause as our attitude towards money. Jesus, in the Gospels, talked about money almost more than any other subject. And why? Because the itch for money is in most palms, and he knew that unless his followers thought clearly about their attachment to their money, they could never become mature disciples.

When we consider material possessions we face a sharp issue, for either we will transform the material into the image of the spiritual or the material will transform us into its own image. Material things must be surrendered to God—if not we will soon find ourselves surrendering to the material. Some Christians give a tenth of their income to God, and for those on low incomes that is a fine thing. Others with higher incomes, however, find they can give away more than a tithe without incurring any hardship for themselves or their families. A businessman put it wisely when he said: "Everything I own is God's, and my constant prayer is this: 'Lord, how much of your money can I keep for myself?'" That is the right priority, for everything we needlessly spend on ourselves prevents us from ministering to the needs of others. Holding our possessions at God's disposal means our trust is in him, not in money.

In a day when economy is preached like a Christian gospel, and generous impulses are throttled before they can find expression, we must allow God to open up our clenched fists and be as generous to others as he is to us. All giving ought to be in gratitude for what he has given to us.

> O God, make me a more generous person. Forgive me
> for my stinginess and infuse me with a desire to minis-
> ter to others in the way that you minister to me. Help
> me not to put it off any longer but to begin today. In
> Jesus' name I ask it, Amen.

WHEN IT'S DIFFICULT TO BE GENEROUS

WHEN SCRIPTURE FAILS TO ─────── COME ALIVE

—A prayer to pray whenever you peruse the Scriptures.
Open my eyes that I may see
    wonderful things in your law. (Ps. 119:18)

—The psalmist's willingness to be exposed.
Search me, O God, and know my heart;
    test me and know my anxious thoughts. (Ps. 139:23)

—Scripture—the life of the soul.
Jesus answered, "It is written: 'Man does not live on bread alone, but
on every word that comes from the mouth of God.'" (Matt. 4:4)

—The Word of God—higher than the word of men.
And we also thank God continually because, when you received the
word of God, which you heard from us, you accepted it not as the
word of men, but as it actually is, the word of God, which is at work
in you who believe. (1 Thess. 2:13)

—The Word of God—a Christian's only offensive weapon.
Take the helmet of salvation and the sword of the Spirit, which is the
word of God. (Eph. 6:17)

—A prayer for understanding.
Let me understand the teaching of your precepts;
    then I will meditate on your wonders. (Ps. 119:27)

—The more one knows the Word, the more one can help others.
I myself am convinced, my brothers, that you yourselves are full of
goodness, complete in knowledge and competent to instruct one
another. (Rom. 15:14)

—The right attitude to approach Scripture.
Let us examine our ways and test them,
and let us return to the LORD. (Lam. 3:40)

21

The Bible, all true Christians would agree, is the most fascinating, engrossing, and sustaining book in the whole world. Hebrews 4:12 describes it in this way: "For the word of God is living and active. Sharper than any double-edged sword, it penetrates even to dividing soul and spirit, joints and marrow; it judges the thoughts and attitudes of the heart." Why then should a Book that is described as "living and active" sometimes fail to impact our lives when we peruse its pages?

There are several reasons why this could be so: reading it too hurriedly, coming to it from a sense of duty rather than to meet with the Author, having our minds preoccupied with many other things. But the major reason why the Bible does not impact our lives is our unwillingness to let it uncover the hidden purposes of our hearts. *We will never really get much out of the Bible until we come to it with exposure in mind.* In other words, we must not be content with just reading the Bible—we must let the Bible read us.

When we approach the Bible in this way we will discover it is more shocking than supportive, more convicting than comforting. That is not to say it does not breathe comfort to us whenever we are in distress, for it most certainly does. Its *main* function, though, is to expose our wrong assumptions about life and to replace them with biblical perspectives. Thus those who invariably have a comfortable time reading the Bible may not be reading it correctly. When we approach the Scriptures with the attitude of heart that says, "Speak Lord, thy servant heareth," the promise of Hebrews 4:12 cannot fail to come true.

> *Father, forgive me for coming to your Word with my defenses intact, bent more on gaining support than being searched. From now on my defenses are down. Help me to trust you to give me what I need. In Christ's name I ask it, Amen.*

WHEN SCRIPTURE FAILS TO COME ALIVE

WHEN SOMEONE CLOSE TO ─────── YOU DIES

—The only one who can hold the soul together.
My comfort in my suffering is this:
   Your promise preserves my life. (Ps. 119:50)

—Feelings must be faced and felt before they can be consoled.
Blessed are those who mourn,
   for they will be comforted. (Matt. 5:4)

—A word that has consoled multitudes.
Even though I walk
   through the valley of the shadow of death,
I will fear no evil,
   for you are with me;
your rod and your staff,
   they comfort me. (Ps. 23:4)

—Immerse yourself in the comfort that comes from God.
Praise be to the God and Father of our Lord Jesus Christ, the Father
of compassion and the God of all comfort, who comforts us in all our
troubles. (2 Cor. 1:3–4)

—A promise that has never been broken.
For in the day of trouble
   he will keep me safe in his dwelling;
he will hide me in the shelter of his tabernacle
   and set me high upon a rock. (Ps. 27:5)

—For this purpose our Lord came.
He has sent me to bind up the brokenhearted . . . to comfort all who
mourn, and provide for those who grieve in Zion—to bestow on them
a crown of beauty instead of ashes, the oil of gladness instead of
mourning, and a garment of praise instead of a spirit of despair.
(Isa. 61:1b–3)

—Death does not have the final word.
"Death has been swallowed up in victory. Where, O death, is your victory? Where, O death, is your sting?" (1 Cor. 15:54b–55)

22

Sooner or later almost every one of us has to face the death of a person we love. However, the comfort of Christ in bereavement is sure. Forgive the personal reference here, but some years ago I lost my wife through cancer and I know what I am about to say is true.

When death takes from our side someone we love, the pain we experience can at times be almost intolerable. We must not be afraid to express our feelings to God (or about him) whatever they may be—fear, hurt, anger, frustration, a sense of abandonment, and so on. These feelings are better expressed than repressed. C. S. Lewis said that when his wife died he railed against God for a while. Then, when he had spent himself in accusations against the Almighty, he sensed the loving arms of God go around him in a way that even he was unable to describe. God is not upset with us when we tell him exactly how we feel; he listens, feels for us, and understands. As soon as possible, though, we must invite him into our pain and draw upon his comforting strength and support.

Divine comfort does not mean that our tears will dry up or our grief will come to a sudden halt. These are natural processes that have a powerful, therapeutic effect. What it does mean is that we will feel God there in the midst of our tears and grief. The pain must be entered into and worked through—even the pain of saying good-bye. Christ's ministry in bereavement is to steer us gently along the path of pain and to walk with us hand in hand, no matter how long the road may be. Never will Christ's presence be more powerful and consoling than it is in bereavement. He gives most when most is taken away.

> O God my Father, how thankful I am to know that
> you accept me as I am. I turn to you in my grief and
> ask that you might put your hand in mine and stay
> close to me as I walk this painful path. Be my true com-
> fort in the midst of my sorrow. In Jesus' name, Amen.

WHEN SOMEONE CLOSE TO
YOU DIES

—Real life is not in temporal things but in God.
Set your minds on things above, not on earthly things. For you died, and your life is now hidden with Christ in God. When Christ, who is your life, appears, then you also will appear with him in glory. (Col. 3:2–4)

—A goal that can never be blocked.
So we make it our goal to please him, whether we are at home in the body or away from it. (2 Cor. 5:9)

—Live always to please the Lord.
Live as children of light (for the fruit of the light consists in all goodness, righteousness and truth) and find out what pleases the Lord. (Eph. 5:8b–10)

—Paul's goals were godly goals.
Brothers, I do not consider myself yet to have taken hold of it. But one thing I do: Forgetting what is behind and straining toward what is ahead, I press on toward the goal to win the prize for which God has called me heavenward in Christ Jesus. (Phil. 3:13–14)

—You're a fool if you get angry.
Do not be quickly provoked in your spirit,
    for anger resides in the lap of fools. (Eccles. 7:9)

—Anger and righteousness are incompatible.
My dear brothers, take note of this: Everyone should be quick to listen, slow to speak and slow to become angry, for man's anger does not bring about the righteous life that God desires. (James 1:19–20)

—Deal with anger the same day it arises.
"In your anger do not sin": Do not let the sun go down while you are still angry, and do not give the devil a foothold. (Eph. 4:26–27)

As there is a good jealousy and a bad jealousy so there is a good anger and a bad anger. Good anger is grief at what is happening to others; bad anger is a grudge at what is happening to us.

Jesus became angry when a group of critics waited to see if he would heal a man in the synagogue. The Bible says: "He looked around at them in anger and deeply distressed" (Mark 3:5). His was a righteous anger, for it consisted of grief that some in the congregation preferred him not to heal because it was the Sabbath.

Unrighteous anger comes about largely from someone or something blocking our goal. Every action we undertake is an attempt to reach a goal that deep down makes good sense to us. When a goal is blocked, *depending on how important the goal seems to us*, the consequent emotion will be either a feeling of mild frustration or blazing anger. It is harmful to deny we are angry; we should *always* acknowledge it and then focus on what is causing the anger. Find out if the underlying cause is that a goal we believe we *must* get to in order to feel inwardly satisfied or fulfilled has been blocked.

The way to avoid incapacitating anger is to see that the obstruction of a goal makes no difference to our security in Christ. And we must know, also, the difference between a desire and a demand. When we simply *desire* something and it is blocked, we are only mildly frustrated. When we *demand* something and it is blocked, we become deeply frustrated. Those whose confidence is in Christ, rather than in the good feelings that come from the achievement of goals, find anger to be no longer an unmanageable issue.

> *Father, help me understand the difference between a desire and a demand, for I see that it is a watershed issue. May I be so secure in you that the blocking of my goals is a minor rather than a major issue. In Jesus' name I pray, Amen.*

WHEN STRUGGLING WITH ANGER ———

~

WHEN PERPLEXED BY THE ———
PROSPERITY OF THE UNGODLY

—Changing one's perspective.
When I tried to understand all this, it was oppressive to me till I entered the sanctuary of God; then I understood their final destiny. (Ps. 73:16–17)

—Ungodliness has no future.
Do not fret because of evil men or be envious of those who do wrong; for like the grass they will soon wither, like green plants they will soon die away. Trust in the LORD and do good; dwell in the land and enjoy safe pasture. (Ps. 37:1–3)

—Only the riches of God survive.
"But God said to him, 'You fool! This very night your life will be demanded from you. Then who will get what you have prepared for yourself?' This is how it will be with anyone who stores up things for himself but is not rich towards God." (Luke 12:20–21)

—Envy is bad for you.
A heart at peace gives life to the body, but envy rots the bones. (Prov. 14:30)

—Earthly things are merely temporary.
I have seen a wicked and ruthless man flourishing like a green tree in its native soil, but he soon passed away and was no more; though I looked for him, he could not be found. (Ps. 37:35–36)

—God's answer to Jeremiah's complaint.
Why does the way of the wicked prosper? Why do all the faithless live at ease? . . . "But if any nation does not listen, I will completely uproot and destroy it," declares the LORD. (Jer. 12:1, 17)

—Zeal, not envy, ought to dominate our hearts.
Do not let your heart envy sinners, but always be zealous for the fear of the LORD. (Prov. 23:17)

—A distinction with a great difference.
And you will again see the distinction between the righteous and the wicked, between those who serve God and those who do not. (Mal. 3:18)

24

Few Christians have not pondered the problem of why it is that ungodly people appear to get away with so much while the good seem to be beset by so many problems. The psalmist voiced this dilemma in Psalm 73. If we were to paraphrase what he said it would sound something like this: "Here I am, living a godly life, keeping my heart and hands clean, avoiding sin, meditating on the Word of God, yet despite this I am facing all kinds of trouble and sorrows. What's the advantage in serving God if he doesn't protect me from the difficulties I am in?" How did the psalmist move through that perplexity to a position of trust and dependency on God? If we can discover that, then perhaps we can emerge with changed perspectives too.

The first thing he did was to go into the house of the Lord, and as he lifted up his eyes to God in worship, his way of looking at things began to change. He saw things from God's perspective, and the matter that seemed to turn him around was this: "Then I understood their final destiny" (v. 17). As soon as he considered the end of the road for the ungodly, everything fell into place for him. He had looked only at their present position—ignoring moral restrictions, pursuing evil ambitions—and had forgotten their destiny. When he understood that, he ceased to be envious and thought to himself: "They might as well be happy now for their end will be one of extreme unhappiness."

The truth that the psalmist saw and held on to as he quietly sat in the house of God is the one we must see and hold on to also. We can always live with the present when we understand and know the future.

> *O Father, how desperately I need the perspectives of Scripture if I am to make my way through this world with calmness and poise. Help me keep my eyes on the future, for I see that only as I do this can I live effectively in the present, Amen.*

WHEN PERPLEXED BY THE PROSPERITY OF THE UNGODLY

WHEN WEIGHED DOWN
BY STRESS

—Keep close to God.
"Take my yoke upon you and learn from me, for I am gentle and humble in heart, and you will find rest for your souls." (Matt. 11:29)

—God alone can keep the mind at peace.
You will keep in perfect peace
    him whose mind is steadfast,
       because he trusts in you. (Isa. 26:3)

—God promises rest for all who trust him.
The LORD replied, "My Presence will go with you, and I will give you rest." (Exod. 33:14)

—Trust God to work things out.
You discern my going out and my lying down;
    you are familiar with all my ways.
Before a word is on my tongue
    you know it completely, O LORD.
You hem me in—behind and before;
    you have laid your hand upon me. (Ps. 139:3–5)

—Follow Christ's directions.
He guides the humble in what is right
    and teaches them his way. (Ps. 25:9)

—Counsel is available for those who stop to listen.
I will instruct you and teach you in the way you should go;
    I will counsel you and watch over you. (Ps. 32:8)

—Don't borrow from tomorrow.
"Therefore do not worry about tomorrow, for tomorrow will worry about itself. Each day has enough trouble of its own." (Matt. 6:34)

—The place to cast all your cares.
Cast your cares on the LORD and he will sustain you; he will never let the righteous fall. (Ps. 55:22)

25

In today's world multitudes of men and women suffer from the effects of stress. One doctor defines stress as "the wear and tear on the personality." Experts on stress tell us it comes from two main causes: too little change and too much change.

To function at peak efficiency we all need a certain amount of change, but when change comes too fast for us to cope with, the personality is put under tremendous pressure. Dr. Thomas Holmes, a recognized authority on stress, measures it in terms of "units of change." The death of a loved one, for example, measures 100 units; a divorce, 73 units; pregnancy, 40 units; moving or refurbishing a home, 25 units; and Christmas is given 12 units. His conclusion is that no one can handle more than 300 units of stress in a twelve-month period without suffering physically or emotionally during the next two years.

The first thing to do when experiencing stress is to identify what is causing it. What is the trigger? Is it too little change or too much? What are the symptoms? What happened immediately prior to the symptoms' occurring? (This can be a vital clue.) We must invite the Lord to help with the matter as we think and pray it through. Only when the cause is found can things be changed.

Next, we must consider why it is that we are victims of stress. Are we unable to move ahead because of fear, or are we going too fast because we are afraid of what we might discover about ourselves if we stopped? To the degree we lack security in God, to that degree we will be motivated to find it in something else. The secure are less prone to stress because they already have what they want—inner peace of mind.

> *Father, help me face up to the issue of where my true*
> *security lies—in things or in you. For I see that the only*
> *way to live without stress in a stressful world is to have*
> *my inner core buttressed by you. Help me, my Father.*
> *In Jesus' name, Amen.*

WHEN WEIGHED DOWN
BY STRESS

~

WHEN SELFISHNESS PREVAILS ———————

—The selflessness of our Savior.
Each of you should look not only to your own interests, but also to the interests of others. Your attitude should be the same as that of Christ Jesus. (Phil. 2:4–5)

—What he is, we must also be.
"A new command I give you: Love one another. As I have loved you, so you must love one another." (John 13:34)

—Can this be said of you?
Dear friend, you are faithful in what you are doing for the brothers, even though they are strangers to you. (3 John 5)

—Putting faith to work.
Share with God's people who are in need. Practice hospitality. (Rom. 12:13)

—Putting others first.
Nobody should seek his own good, but the good of others. (1 Cor. 10:24)

—True other-centeredness.
For you know the grace of our Lord Jesus Christ, that though he was rich, yet for your sakes he became poor, so that you through his poverty might become rich. (2 Cor. 8:9)

—We lose what we hold on to.
"For whoever wants to save his life will lose it, but whoever loses his life for me will find it." (Matt. 16:25)

—Self-giving—the hallmark of Christianity.
And live a life of love, just as Christ loved us and gave himself up for us as a fragrant offering and sacrifice to God. (Eph. 5:2)

26

The root cause of most of our problems, many Christian counselors believe, is to be found in selfishness and self-centeredness. Who hasn't been astonished in moments of honest self-examination to discover how much of what we do has a self-reference? To the things that happen around us, isn't our instinctive reaction to say to ourselves, "How will this affect *me*?" We are often more distressed by a trifling mishap that concerns us than a major tragedy that befalls someone else. Selfishness and self-centeredness are so natural to us that it is only when we *make* ourselves face it that the full horror of it comes home.

There is little we can do to correct this distortion of our nature by ourselves, and this is why we must turn to Christ for help. Our Lord's first thoughts were never of himself, and he alone can help us love as he loved. Christianity recognizes the legitimacy of self-love just so long as it is not love *only* for the self, is not sought singly, and is never divorced from equal love of others. When we read the Gospels we do not find one occasion for which our Lord could be convicted of selfishness. Even when facing crucifixion, Christ's thoughts were of forgiveness for those who were crucifying him. He saved Peter, three-times-denying Peter, by a look, and paused to say to the women who lined the path to Calvary, "Do not weep for me; weep for yourselves and for your children" (Luke 23:28).

Selfishness arises out of insecurity—the feeling that we have nothing to give away. Only a close, deep, and ongoing relationship with Christ can overwhelm our natural self-interest and move us from self-centeredness to other-centeredness.

> *O God, help me break this cycle of self-concern and*
> *self-interest. As I bow before you now, overwhelm my*
> *self-centered love with your other-centered love. Break*
> *me, melt me, mold me, and fill me—with Calvary love.*
> *In Jesus' name I ask it, Amen.*

WHEN SELFISHNESS PREVAILS ———

~

WHEN DOWNCAST AND DEPRESSED ———

—Tell yourself the truth.
Why are you downcast, O my, soul? Why so disturbed within me? Put your hope in God, for I will yet praise him, my Savior and my God. (Ps. 42:5–6)

—Only God can give us what our souls long for.
O God, you are my God, earnestly I seek you; my soul thirsts for you, my body longs for you, in a dry and weary land where there is no water. (Ps. 63:1)

—God is closer than you think.
The LORD is close to the brokenhearted and saves those who are crushed in spirit. (Ps. 34:18)

—A prayer pattern to follow.
To you, O LORD, I lift up my soul; in you I trust, O my God. Do not let me be put to shame, nor let my enemies triumph over me. (Ps. 25:1–2)

—You're a child of God—hold on to that.
For you did not receive a spirit that makes you a slave again to fear, but you received the Spirit of sonship. And by him we cry, *"Abba, Father."* The Spirit himself testifies with our spirit that we are God's children. (Rom. 8:15–16)

—Our trials are worth more than they cost.
In this you greatly rejoice, though now for a little while you may have had to suffer grief in all kinds of trials. These have come so that your faith—of greater worth than gold, which perishes even though refined by fire—may be proved genuine and may result in praise, glory and honor when Jesus Christ is revealed. (1 Pet. 1:6–7)

—The best place to run and hide.
You are my hiding-place; you will protect me from trouble and surround me with songs of deliverance. (Ps. 32:7)

Almost everyone, from time to time, will confess to feelings of depression, but usually these feelings quickly pass. When they continue for a few weeks, however, and become increasingly acute, then medical opinion should be sought, if only to ascertain whether or not the cause is physical.

Many things can plunge us into a low mood: uncertainty about the future, a breakdown in relationships, financial difficulties, aging, lack of purpose, and so on. The common denominator, though, with deeply depressed feelings is a sense of loss. It is important to identify the loss, as the mere fact of clarifying it has a curative effect. The loss could even be that of self-esteem, a feeling that one is no longer of value.

A vital clue also to understanding what plunges us into depression is found when we examine the relationship between what we are doing and the expected rewards. If our actions and behaviors do not, over a period of time, bring us the rewards we expect then we can become so discouraged that we sink into a low mood.

The best remedy for all nonbiological depression is to gain a new perspective—to turn one's gaze from earth to heaven. And the most powerful passage in the Bible that addresses the needs of the depressed is Psalm 42. The psalmist saw that there was a thirst inside him that no one could meet except God. When he looked to God for the satisfaction of that thirst (rather than to others), his soul then rested on the hope that no matter what happened, he remained secure as a person. Understanding this and constantly reminding ourselves of it is the key to overcoming and remaining free from depression.

> *O God, help me see that to turn my thoughts heavenward when downcast and depressed may be difficult but not impossible. Show me even more clearly how to have my deep inner thirst met by you. Give me the hope the psalmist had. In Jesus' name I pray, Amen.*

WHEN DOWNCAST AND DEPRESSED ———

WHEN YOU DOUBT THAT GOD IS GOOD

—The truth about God in a nutshell.
For God so loved the world that he gave his one and only Son, that whoever believes in him shall not perish but have eternal life. (John 3:16)

—It is God's goodness that prompts repentance.
Or do you show contempt for the riches of his kindness, tolerance and patience, not realizing that God's kindness leads you toward repentance? (Rom. 2:4)

—Goodness is what God is all about.
"Why do you call me good?" Jesus answered. "No one is good—except God alone." (Mark 10:18)

—The proof of God's goodness.
This is love: not that we loved God, but that he loved us and sent his Son as an atoning sacrifice for our sins. (1 John 4:10)

—God's goodness—the focal point of worship.
When all the Israelites saw the fire coming down and the glory of the LORD above the temple, they knelt on the pavement with their faces to the ground, and they worshiped and gave thanks to the LORD, saying, "He is good; his love endures forever." (2 Chron. 7:3)

—God's goodness underlies the whole creation.
For everything God created is good, and nothing is to be rejected if it is received with thanksgiving. (1 Tim. 4:4)

—You've tasted God's goodness; crave for more.
Like newborn babies, crave pure spiritual milk, so that by it you may grow up in your salvation, now that you have tasted that the Lord is good. (1 Pet. 2:2–3).

—Let the psalmist's affirmation become yours.
The LORD is good to all; he has compassion on all he has made. (Ps. 145:9)

28

"The root of sin," said Oswald Chambers, "is the belief that God is not good." There are a multitude of circumstances and events we have to face in a fallen world that suggest that God is not good: earthquakes, famines, storms, and floods that wipe out whole communities, disease, and so on.

Before radar was invented, the art of navigation depended on the existence of fixed points. Mariners took their bearings not from a cloud or a floating spar but from the stars and from things that were solid, such as a headland or a lighthouse. If a seaman took a bearing and found he was off course, he would not doubt the star or the headland—he would doubt himself.

We need to do the same whenever we find ourselves doubting that God is good. We must see to it that we are fixed to the things that are fixed. The Cross is one of those things. It is the *irrefutable* proof that God is love. When we look around and consider the many situations that seem to belie the fact that God is love, we must not pretend these matters do not cause us problems. Rather, we must set them all over against the one thing that is crystal clear—God's love as demonstrated for us on Calvary. A God who would do that for us simply must be Love. At the foot of Calvary the ground is fixed. We do not have there the answers to everything, but we see enough of God to be able to trust him, and thus say with the poet:

> Here in the maddening maze of things
> When tossed by storm and flood
> To one fixed ground my spirit clings
> I know that God is good.

O Father, help me whenever I am tempted to think otherwise to focus on the irrefutable fact of your love for me poured out at Calvary. Show me how to work from the clear to the unclear, not the other way around. In Jesus' name I ask it, Amen.

WHEN YOU DOUBT THAT ———
GOD IS GOOD

WHEN FACING BITTER ——————
DISAPPOINTMENT

—All things serve.
And we know that in all things God works for the good of those who love him, who have been called according to his purpose. (Rom: 8:28)

—Hand over to God your deep concern.
Cast all your anxiety on him because he cares for you. (1 Pet. 5:7)

—Stand—even though you do not understand.
A man's steps are directed by the LORD.
    How then can anyone understand his own way? (Prov. 20:24)

—From God alone comes the strength to stand.
You are awesome, O God, in your sanctuary;
    the God of Israel gives power and strength to his people.
    (Ps. 68:35)

—God's power shows up best in weak people.
But he said to me, "My grace is sufficient for you, for my power is made perfect in weakness." Therefore I will boast all the more gladly about my weaknesses, so that Christ's power may rest on me. (2 Cor. 12:9)

—A steadfast mind is a mind focused on God.
You will keep in perfect peace
    him whose mind is steadfast,
    because he trusts in you. (Isa. 26:3)

—Recognize that God always knows best.
In his heart a man plans his course,
    but the LORD determines his steps. (Prov. 16:9)

—God reigns even when circumstances suggest the opposite.
Then I heard what sounded like a great multitude, like the roar of rushing waters and like loud peals of thunder, shouting: "Hallelujah! For our Lord God Almighty reigns." (Rev. 19:6)

29

Hardly any of us can go through life without experiencing on occasions the dampening effect of disappointment. A friend we hoped would come through for us lets us down; an event on which we pinned a great deal of hope fails to materialize; an important promise made to us is broken. Dealing with such disappointments is not easy. The following three principles, however, when followed and practiced, should help.

First, we must accept that what has happened has happened. When, in the effort to get away from the pain of disappointment, we pretend that something has not happened, or that it has happened in a different way, we deceive ourselves. Integrity requires that whatever is true, whatever is real, must be faced.

Second, we must acknowledge our feelings. If we feel hurt, angry, frustrated, or any other negative emotion, we must be willing to face them. Unacknowledged emotions invariably cause trouble.

Third, we must bring the issue to God in prayer, remembering that he can take every one of life's disappointments and make them work for us rather than against us (Rom. 8:28–29). Just change the first letter of *disappointment* from *D* to *H* and *disappointment* becomes *His-appointment*. A Christian poet put the same truth like this:

> Deep in unfathomable mines
> Of never-failing skill
> He treasures up his bright designs
> And works his Sovereign will.

Father, thank you for reminding me of your skill at turning blocks into blessings. Forgive me for ever doubting it. Help me believe that even this disappointment will be taken by you and made to serve. Thank you, dear Father. In Jesus' name, Amen.

WHEN FACING BITTER DISAPPOINTMENT

WHEN LACKING SPIRITUAL ─────── ASSURANCE

—A fact that can be depended upon.
If we confess our sins, he is faithful and just and will forgive us our sins and purify us from all unrighteousness. (1 John 1:9)

—Access to God is by faith, not feeling.
Therefore, since we have been justified through faith, we have peace with God through our Lord Jesus Christ, through whom we have gained access by faith into this grace in which we now stand. (Rom. 5:1–2)

—Salvation—a gift to receive.
For it is by grace you have been saved, through faith—and this not from yourselves, it is the gift of God—not by works, so that no one can boast. (Eph. 2:8–9)

—Heartfelt contrition is never ignored.
The sacrifices of God are a broken spirit;
    a broken and contrite heart,
    O God, you will not despise. (Ps. 51:17)

—Is this what is holding things up?
"For if you forgive men when they sin against you, your heavenly Father will also forgive you. But if you do not forgive men their sins, your Father will not forgive your sins." (Matt. 6:14–15)

—A solemn but necessary warning.
"This is how my heavenly Father will treat each of you unless you forgive your brother from your heart." (Matt. 18:35)

—You offer yourself for salvation; Christ will complete it.
Therefore he is able to save completely those who come to God through him, because he always lives to intercede for them. (Heb. 7:25)

30

More Christians suffer from lack of spiritual assurance than we might at first think. Despite having made a commitment to Christ, they don't *feel* saved, and this prompts the question: Did God not hear me when I invited him to come into my life? Three things usually contribute to a lack of spiritual assurance.

First, we put an undue emphasis on feelings. Although salvation generally makes an impact upon the emotions, the absence of strong feelings does not indicate one is unsaved. Forgiveness of sins and the entering of one's name in the Lamb's book of life is done on the basis of commitment, not feeling. Nothing can be more explicit in Scripture than that Christ received sinners. "Come to me . . . ," he said, "and I will give you rest" (Matt. 11:28). "Whoever comes to me I will never drive away" (John 6:37).

Second, we may not have fully repented when we made our initial commitment to Christ. Repentance is more than asking God to forgive our sins; it also involves surrendering the ego at his feet. The ego is the core of our self-centeredness, and until we agree before God that he is to be central and our ego marginal, we have not properly repented.

Third, we may block the flow of God's forgiveness to us by our unwillingness to forgive others. When we hold bitterness and resentment against others, we raise an obstacle against God's forgiveness of us. It is not that God won't forgive us, but that his forgiveness can't reach the deep parts of our soul because of the self-erected barriers. Consider these points, take whatever steps are necessary, and as surely as night follows day, spiritual assurance will flow through.

> Gracious and loving heavenly Father, your truth is like
> a searchlight to my soul. Help me think these issues
> through right now and apply any necessary correctives.
> In Christ's peerless and all-prevailing name I pray,
> Amen.

WHEN LACKING SPIRITUAL ASSURANCE

WHEN AFRAID OF DEATH ———————

—Death met its defeat in Christ.
"Where, O death, is your victory? Where, O death, is your sting?" The sting of death is sin, and the power of sin is the law. But thanks be to God! He gives us the victory through our Lord Jesus Christ. (1 Cor. 15:55–57)

—Death in Adam, life in Christ.
For as in Adam all die, so in Christ all will be made alive. (1 Cor. 15:22)

—Other things may perish, but never a Christian.
"I give them eternal life, and they shall never perish; no one can snatch them out of my hand." (John 10:28)

—Your Lord is waiting to meet you.
And if I go and prepare a place for you, I will come back and take you to be with me that you also may be where I am. (John 14:3)

—Immortality—the fabric of the righteous soul.
In the way of righteousness there is life;
    along that path is immortality. (Prov. 12:28)

—The death of death.
    He will swallow up death forever.
The Sovereign LORD will wipe away the tears
    from all faces;
he will remove the disgrace of his people
    from all the earth. The LORD has spoken. (Isa. 25:8)

—Hold on to this—millions have done so before you.
Even though I walk through the valley of the shadow of death, I will fear no evil, for you are with me; your rod and your staff, they comfort me. (Ps. 23:4)

—What you are hereafter depends on what you are after here.
The world and its desires pass away, but the man who does the will of God lives forever. (1 John 2:17)

31

All sane people, to varying degrees, have a fear of death. "It is as old as human life," says one writer, "as long as human life and as widespread as human life." We shall all die. If men and women did not have some fear of death then suicide would be far more common than it is. It is a natural fear. Christian studies on the subject of death show three underlying concerns: (1) the physical fact of dying, (2) the fear of finality, (3) the fear of judgment. Not all three elements are always present, and one or two elements may be stronger in some than others.

People fear the physical fact of dying because of the possibility of great pain, but the beneficent power of modern drugs makes the chances of this remote. A number of thanatologists (people who conduct research into the stages of dying) say that the struggle some people demonstrate in death is largely unconscious and is more agonizing for those looking on than for the person concerned.

The second fear—the fear of finality—need not concern a Christian. Death does not end all. The resurrection of our Lord proves that the spiritual part of us survives death, and that it was death that died, not he.

The third fear—the fear of judgment—is not as strong as it once was in human minds. This is due in no small measure to the fact that fewer people attend church and that teaching on the final judgment seems in some churches (not all) to be nonexistent. No man or woman who knows Christ need fear judgment. God has consumed our sin and incinerated it at Calvary. Our Lord stands as a great wall between penitent sinners and their sin. We simply *must* rejoice in that.

> Gracious and loving Lord, drive this truth deep within
> me. Help me never forget that all that death does is to
> usher me into the Father's immediate presence and give
> me an abiding place in the great company of the
> redeemed. I am so thankful, Amen.

WHEN AFRAID OF DEATH

WHEN YOU NEED DIVINE ───── GUIDANCE

—Humility—a prerequisite of divine guidance.
He guides the humble in what is right
  and teaches them his way. (Ps. 25:9)

—Have no will of your own.
Trust in the LORD with all your heart and lean not on your own understanding; in all your ways acknowledge him, and he will make your paths straight. (Prov. 3:5–6)

—Why sometimes guidance is unclear.
You do not have, because you do not ask God. When you ask, you do not receive, because you ask with wrong motives, that you may spend what you get on your pleasures. (James 4:2b–3)

—How to pray for guidance.
Show me your ways, O LORD, teach me your paths; guide me in your truth and teach me, for you are God my Savior, and my hope is in you all day long. (Ps. 25:4–5)

—A further emphasis on humility.
Good and upright is the LORD; therefore he instructs sinners in his ways. He guides the humble in what is right and teaches them his way. (Ps. 25:8–9)

—A committed life is a guided life.
Commit your way to the LORD; trust in him and he will do this. (Ps. 37:5)

—Guidance—all the way to glory.
You guide me with your counsel, and afterward you will take me into glory. (Ps. 73:24)

—He guides until we will no longer need it.
For this God is our God for ever and ever; he will be our guide even to the end. (Ps. 48:14)

32

Few Christians have difficulty believing in the personal guidance of God. For the most part our difficulty is not with the fact *that* God guides but *how*. Usually God guides along five main routes: (1) through prayerful reading of the Scriptures, (2) through the preaching of God's Word, (3) through reason, (4) through circumstances, and (5) through a strong inner witness. How do these all come together when we are in need of personal guidance?

First, we need to surrender our own likes or dislikes to God in prayer and determine to have no will of our own in the matter. Our desire should be: "Not my will but Thine be done." A twenty-four-hour period of fasting also helps as it can tune the spirit and sensitize it to hearing God's voice more clearly. People have found God's guidance while prayerfully reading his Word, as a certain verse is quickened to them. Others have heard his voice through a sermon in church.

Still others find the divine will by reasoning an issue through, either by themselves or with a godly friend or counselor. Circumstances can point the way to God's will also. Things may get chaotic, but often God shakes our circumstances to move us in a different direction.

Then finally there is what some Christians call the *way of peace*. To find guidance it can help to look at the various options open to you, then picture yourself going down them one by one. On one of these paths a deeper peace may rest; not a thrill, not pleasure, but *peace*. This may be the road down which God wants you to travel. Remember, however, it's always good to share all your conclusions about God's guidance, if you can, with a wise and godly friend.

> O God, with so many paths to guidance I see that my problem is not that you are failing to speak but that I am not hearing. Help me be more prayerful, more sensitive, more alert, and more ready to do your will. In Christ's name I ask it, Amen.

WHEN YOU NEED DIVINE ——— GUIDANCE

WHEN PAINFUL MEMORIES ————
PERSIST

—Forgive as you have been forgiven.
Bear with each other and forgive whatever grievances you may have against one another. Forgive as the Lord forgave you. (Col. 3:13)

—Unforgiveness blocks God's work in you.
"And when you stand praying, if you hold anything against anyone, forgive him, so that your Father in heaven may forgive you your sins." (Mark 11:25)

—Forgiveness must be without measure.
Then Peter came to Jesus and asked, "Lord, how many times shall I forgive my brother when he sins against me? Up to seven times?" Jesus answered, "I tell you, not seven times, but seventy-seven times." (Matt. 18:21–22)

—Forget techniques; trust in God to make you whole.
Who among you fears the LORD and obeys the word of his servant? Let him who walks in the dark, who has no light, trust in the name of the LORD and rely on his God. (Isa. 50:10)

—No one but God can restore the soul.
   He restores my soul.
He guides me in paths of righteousness
   for his name's sake. (Ps. 23:3)

—No one has been hurt more than our Lord.
Because he himself suffered when he was tempted, he is able to help those who are being tempted. (Heb. 2:18)

—Christ knows exactly how we feel.
For we do not have a high priest who is unable to sympathize with our weaknesses, but we have one who has been tempted in every way, just as we are—yet was without sin. (Heb. 4:15)

—Be an overcomer.
Do not be overcome by evil, but overcome evil with good. (Rom. 12:21)

33

In today's Christian community a great emphasis is being placed on dealing with painful or disturbing memories. But not all the theories being offered to deal with this problem are in keeping with the Scriptures. Some suggest that painful memories (such as memories of deep horror or severe hurt) can be obliterated. They can't. We cannot ever completely forget what has been done to us, but what God is able to do is remove the burning sensation that accompanies hurtful memories and deliver us from their cutting acuteness.

Before we ask God to deal with any disturbing memories of the past, we ought to consider very carefully the possibility of hatred and bitterness being resident in our hearts as a consequence of what has happened to us. Some theories of counseling encourage people to picture in their minds the person who hurt them or abused them and vent their hatred or bitterness on them in an imaginary way. This is a technique that is in conflict with Scripture. The Bible encourages us to forgive our enemies, not rail against them. When forgiveness flows from the heart, then the condition is right to invite God to remove from the memory all sense of hurt or shame.

Consider how God did this with Joseph. Though he had been flung into a pit, sold by his own brothers, slandered by a lascivious woman, and thrust into prison, there came a time when all this was behind him, and he realized after his firstborn son arrived that God had *made* him forget (Gen. 41:51). It was not that his memories of the past had been expunged. It was rather that the sharp edge had come off them. And what God did for Joseph he can do also for you.

> *O Father, through and by your grace I offer forgiveness to all those who have ever hurt me or abused me. Take each one of my hurting memories and remove the pain. Minister your love and healing to me in the name that is above every name—the name of Jesus, Amen.*

WHEN PAINFUL MEMORIES PERSIST

—It's important to face and feel negative emotions.
When I heard these things, I sat down and wept. For some days I mourned and fasted and prayed before the God of heaven. (Neh. 1:4)

—Confess and admit your own failures.
"Why do you look at the speck of sawdust in your brother's eye and pay no attention to the plank in your own eye? . . . First take the plank out of your own eye, and then you will see clearly to remove the speck from your brother's eye." (Matt. 7:3, 5)

—Give all your expectations to God.
Find rest, O my soul, in God alone; my hope comes from him. (Ps. 62:5)

—Hold fast to this truth.
And we know that in all things God works for the good of those who love him, who have been called according to his purpose. (Rom. 8:28)

—Deepen your relationship with God.
Since, then, you have been raised with Christ, set your hearts on things above, where Christ is seated at the right hand of God. Set your minds on things above, not on earthly things. For you died, and your life is now hidden with Christ in God. (Col. 3:1–3)

—Claim God's forgiveness for any relational failures.
Have mercy on me, O God,
    according to your unfailing love;
according to your great compassion
    blot out my transgressions. (Ps. 51:1)

—Forgive your partner as God forgives you.
But if you do not forgive men their sins, your Father will not forgive your sins. (Matt. 6:15)

—Rebuild with God.
Your people will rebuild the ancient ruins and will raise up the age-old foundations; you will be called Repairer of Broken Walls, Restorer of Streets with Dwellings. (Isa. 58:12)

The breakup of a marriage can be more traumatic and painful than even the death of one's partner. In death one says good-bye, and after a period of grief and mourning the heart gathers new strength and feels alive once again. But a separation or divorce takes a toll that is hard to describe. Friends can help and be a great support, but there is no one who understands like Jesus. He knows, more than anyone else, what it means to be misunderstood, rejected, and hurt. Taking the steps outlined here will not be easy, but experience has shown that when they are followed, the strength to persevere and continue with life is revived.

First, talk to God about the matter. It is vitally important to acknowledge to yourself and to God all your hurt or angry feelings. Hurt cannot be healed until it is recognized. Next, search the Scriptures daily, asking God to give you words of encouragement. God quickens different Scriptures to different people. The Psalms can be of special help in this connection. Third, come to terms, painful though it may be, with the fact your marriage *may* not be restored. If there is hope that it may, then live in that hope, but also in the knowledge that it may not.

Fourth, remind yourself that you are first a person before being a partner. Though a *partnership* may be broken, your identity as a person *in Christ* cannot. Fifth, develop a close and continuing relationship with God in prayer. Being bereft of a partner brings a certain loneliness, but it provides an opportunity for knowing God in a way you might never have known him before.

> *Loving heavenly Father, if ever I have needed your*
> *strength and grace it is now. As you have helped others*
> *in this same position, help me I pray. I offer my heart*
> *with all its pain to you. Touch me, heal me, and revive*
> *my flagging spirit. In Jesus' name I ask it, Amen.*

WHEN A MARRIAGE FAILS ———————

———————————————————

———————————————————

———————————————————

———————————————————

———————————————————

———————————————————

———————————————————

———————————————————

———————————————————

———————————————————

———————————————————

———————————————————

———————————————————

———————————————————

———————————————————

———————————————————

———————————————————

———————————————————

———————————————————

———————————————————

———————————————————

———————————————————

———————————————————

———————————————————

———————————————————

~

WHEN YOU FEEL FORGOTTEN ——————
BY GOD

—God has promised never to forget you.
"Can a mother forget the baby at her breast
    and have no compassion on the child she has borne?
Though she may forget,
    I will not forget you!" (Isa. 49:15)

—God's name is at stake in this.
For the sake of his great name the LORD will not reject his people,
because the LORD was pleased to make you his own. (1 Sam. 12:22)

—Your family may forget you, but God never will.
Though my father and mother forsake me,
    the LORD will receive me. (Ps. 27:10)

—God will never forsake his own.
For the LORD loves the just
    and will not forsake his faithful ones.
They will be protected forever,
    but the offspring of the wicked will be cut off. (Ps. 37:28)

—Never means never.
Be content with what you have, because God has said, "Never will I
leave you; never will I forsake you." (Heb. 13:5b)

—The "Never" promise reinforced.
No one will be able to stand up against you all the days of your life.
As I was with Moses, so I will be with you; I will never leave you nor
forsake you. (Josh. 1:5)

—Nothing escapes God's attention.
He will not let your foot slip—
    he who watches over you will not slumber;
indeed, he who watches over Israel
    will neither slumber nor sleep. (Ps. 121:3–4)

—If God can't forget a sparrow—can he forget you?
"Are not five sparrows sold for two pennies? Yet not one of them is
forgotten by God." (Luke 12:6)

35

It is forgivable, when overtaken by all kinds of difficulties and problems, to think that we are forgotten by God. Forgivable, but not true.

From observation and experience it appears that the Christians who fall prey to this misapprehension are those who struggle with a deep sense of inferiority and see themselves as being of little consequence on this earth. Feeling of little importance on earth, they deduce, erroneously, that they are of little importance in heaven. The psalmist reminded us in Psalm 139 that God's thoughts are always towards us and that they are more in number than the grains of sand (v. 18).

But perhaps the greatest verse we can focus our attention on when we are tempted to think that God has forgotten us is Isaiah 49:16: "See, I have engraved you on the palms of my hands." The palm of the hand has passed into our proverbs as a symbol of familiarity. We sometimes hear people say: "I know it like the palm of my hand." It is on the palm of his hand, said the prophet Isaiah, that God has put our names. And they are not just written there, but *engraved* there. This means our names are before him in such a way that they cannot be overlooked. He does not depend on a ministering spirit to bring our names to his attention. They are imprinted there—on the palms of his hands. The hymnist put it powerfully when he wrote:

> See where before the throne he stands
> And pours the all-prevailing prayer;
> Points to his side and lifts his hands
> And shows that you are graven there!
> Graven there! Never forget it.

O Father, what a comfort it is to know that the great
God who sustains this universe thinks about me. The
Lord of Life watches over me and cannot ever forget
me, for I am graven on the palms of his hands. Thank
you, my Father, Thank you. Amen.

WHEN YOU FEEL FORGOTTEN ———
BY GOD

WHEN THERE ARE DIFFICULTIES ———
AT HOME

—Life is in Christ, not in others.
Since, then, you have been raised with Christ, set your hearts on things above, where Christ is seated at the right hand of God. Set your minds on things above, not on earthly things. For you died, and your life is now hidden with Christ in God. (Col. 3:1–3)

—God alone can meet your deepest needs.
And my God will meet all your needs according to his glorious riches in Christ Jesus. (Phil. 4:19)

—This kind of love is given, not manufactured.
Love is patient, love is kind. It does not envy, it does not boast, it is not proud. It is not rude, it is not self-seeking, it is not easily angered, it keeps no record of wrongs. (1 Cor. 13:4–5)

—The standard is high, but let God lift you up to it.
Love must be sincere. Hate what is evil; cling to what is good. Be devoted to one another in brotherly love. Honor one another above yourselves. (Rom. 12:9–10)

—A word for husbands.
However, each one of you also must love his wife as he loves himself, and the wife must respect her husband. (Eph. 5:33)

—A word for wives.
Wives, in the same way be submissive to your husbands so that, if any of them do not believe the word, they may be won over without words by the behavior of their wives, when they see the purity and reverence of your lives. (1 Pet. 3:1–2)

—A word for all.
Make every effort to live in peace with all men and to be holy; without holiness no one will see the Lord. See to it that no one misses the grace of God and that no bitter root grows up to cause trouble and defile many. (Heb. 12:14–15)

36

"Life," as Hemingway put it, "breaks us all," but few things are as painful as being broken by difficult circumstances in the home. What kind of troubles bring us to the breaking point in the home? An unfaithful or unloving partner, disobedient or rebellious children, constant bickering and arguments, misunderstandings, financial pressures, living with difficult in-laws, infirmity or sickness, and so on. Many, out of loyalty to their families, face the world with a smile, but inwardly they are torn and bleeding.

A study made at the University of Rhode Island some years ago concluded that one of the most dangerous places on this planet is the average American home. And there is some evidence to show that Europe is quickly catching up.

To survive the problems that can arise in the home we must first be secure in our identity as a person; only then can we be secure as a partner or a parent. If we draw our life and energy from those with whom we are in a relationship rather than from God, then when difficulties arise we will soon find ourselves spiritually bankrupt. No wife, husband, father, mother, son, or daughter, is able to meet the deep needs of our soul; quite simply they are not enough. God is the only one able to do that. It is from him and him alone that we are able to draw the energy and strength to relate well to others. When we attempt to draw that energy from others and not him, we quickly run out of coping ability. The secret of handling all relational problems is to maintain a close, strong, and meaningful relationship with Christ. It will not guarantee that others will change, but it will enable us to cope with everything that comes.

> *Father, I see that you and you alone have the resources I need to cope with life's difficulties and relate well to others. I come to you now for help. Your promise is that as I draw nigh to you, you will draw nigh to me. Strengthen me, I pray. In Jesus' name, Amen.*

WHEN THERE ARE DIFFICULTIES ———
AT HOME

WHEN BATTLING WITH ——————
SEXUAL FRUSTRATION

—Service in the highest degree.
I consider everything a loss compared to the surpassing greatness of knowing Christ Jesus my Lord, for whose sake I have lost all things. I consider them rubbish, that I may gain Christ and be found in him. (Phil. 3:8–9)

—Decide whom and what you will serve.
Do not offer the parts of your body to sin, as instruments of wickedness, but rather offer yourselves to God, as those who have been brought from death to life; and offer the parts of your body to him as instruments of righteousness. (Rom. 6:13)

—Dedicate your whole being to God.
Therefore, I urge you, brothers, in view of God's mercy, to offer your bodies as living sacrifices, holy and pleasing to God—this is your spiritual act of worship. (Rom. 12:1)

—On being a slave to righteousness.
I put this in human terms because you are weak in your natural selves. Just as you used to offer the parts of your body in slavery to impurity and to ever-increasing wickedness, so now offer them in slavery to righteousness leading to holiness. (Rom. 6:19)

—Don't fight—flee.
Flee from sexual immorality. All other sins a man commits are outside his body, but he who sins sexually sins against his own body. Do you not know that your body is a temple of the Holy Spirit, who is in you, whom you have received from God? You are not your own; you were bought at a price. Therefore honor God with your body. (1 Cor. 6:18–20)

—The passion that overcomes every other passion.
"Love the Lord your God with all your heart and with all your soul and with all your mind and with all your strength." (Mark 12:30)

37

The hunger for sex, we must recognize, is no more shameful than the hunger for food. However, this should not be taken to mean that, like the hunger for food, it must be indulged. We can't live without food, but we can live without sex.

The main problem underlying sexual frustration is that of the release of sexual energy. With married people this can be done legitimately through the act of sexual intercourse, but for single people this is forbidden by Scripture. How do single people, and in some circumstances married people also, handle a clamant sex drive? Is masturbation the answer? Scripture is silent on this issue (except for the debatable case of Onan in Gen. 38:9), and some feel that when no other relief can be found, masturbation is permissible, providing no sexual images are being entertained.

There is "a more excellent way," though—the way of sublimation. Sublimation is the rechannelling of energies into another and higher level of activity. One of the best practitioners of this was the apostle Paul. He was obviously unmarried (1 Cor. 7:7), yet although denied biological expression of his sex drive he was not frustrated, as *all* of his energies were harnessed to the cause of God's kingdom. He was creative at the place of the mind and spirit, thus his lower drives were being sublimated.

When all the energies of the spirit are focused on Christ and his kingdom, sexual energies will not be eliminated, but they will be prevented from being a cause of frustration. Many single persons with a strong sex drive have found that it loses its persistent power when they lose themselves in strong service for the Master.

> *Gracious and loving Father, help me learn the art of sublimation—taking what is blocked at a lower level and expressing it at a higher level. I see that the strongly sexed can strongly serve. I dedicate now my whole being to your cause. Amen.*

WHEN BATTLING WITH SEXUAL FRUSTRATION

~

WHEN HARASSED BY FIERCE TEMPTATIONS

—With every temptation there is a way out.
No temptation has seized you except what is common to man. And God is faithful; he will not let you be tempted beyond what you can bear. But when you are tempted, he will also provide a way out so that you can stand up under it. (1 Cor. 10:13)

—Remember too there is always a divine Helper.
Because he himself suffered when he was tempted, he is able to help those who are being tempted. (Heb. 2:18)

—God does not tempt.
When tempted, no one should say, "God is tempting me." For God cannot be tempted by evil, nor does he tempt anyone; but each one is tempted when, by his own evil desire, he is dragged away and enticed. Then, after desire has conceived, it gives birth to sin; and sin, when it is full-grown, gives birth to death. (James 1:13–15)

—Learn to love God more and the world less.
Do not love the world or anything in the world. If anyone loves the world, the love of the Father is not in him. For everything in the world—the cravings of sinful man, the lust of his eyes and the boasting of what he has and does—comes not from the Father but from the world. (1 John 2:15–16)

—Lack self-discipline, and you might live to regret it.
If your hand or your foot causes you to sin, cut it off and throw it away. It is better for you to enter life maimed or crippled than to have two hands or two feet and be thrown into eternal fire. (Matt. 18:8)

—Don't neglect your prayer life.
"Watch and pray so that you will not fall into temptation. The spirit is willing, but the body is weak." (Matt. 26:41)

—Equip yourself with God's resources against temptation.
Put on the full armor of God so that you can take your stand against the devil's schemes. (Eph. 6:11)

38

I once heard a Christian say (somewhat facetiously of course) that he could stand anything except temptation! But for many, temptation is no laughing matter. Temptation can be harassing, yet we ought not to think of it as something entirely negative. The Greek word usually used for temptation in the New Testament is *peirasmos*, which means "to test, to try," or "to prove." There is no question of entrapment or seduction on the part of God in allowing us to be tempted; he permits it to come in order to strengthen us and equip us for more effective service in his kingdom. When Jesus went into the wilderness it was said that he went in "full of the Holy Spirit" (Luke 4:1), but he came out "in the power of the Spirit" (Luke 4:14). Mere fullness had turned to power under the pressure of temptation. Our Lord's spiritual tissues had been strengthened in the struggle.

No matter how strong and fierce the temptations that beset us, we have the firm promise in Scripture that God will engineer a way of escape. Listen to how the apostle Paul put it in 1 Corinthians 10:13: "God is faithful; he will not let you be tempted beyond what you can bear. . . . he will also provide a way out so that you can stand up under it."

How does the Almighty provide us with a way of escape (or as the NIV puts it, "a way out") when harassed by oppressive temptations? He does it by infusing us with the strength and power to resist. There will never be a moment in our lives when God's grace and empowerment are unable to match (and surpass) the power of temptation. This means there is always, *always*, a way out.

> *Father, help me to take my eyes off myself and to turn them to you in the midst of these buffeting temptations. I know that every battle one wins makes the next one easier. Thank you for your unfailing strength and power. I avail myself of it now. In Jesus' name, Amen.*

WHEN HARASSED BY FIERCE TEMPTATIONS

WHEN GOD'S PROMISES ARE DELAYED

—God knows what he is doing.
As for God, his way is perfect;
    the word of the LORD is flawless.
He is a shield
    for all who take refuge in him. (Ps. 18:30)

—God is as good as his Word.
For no matter how many promises God has made, they are "Yes" in Christ. And so through him the "Amen" is spoken by us to the glory of God. (2 Cor. 1:20)

—God can do anything but fail.
"Praise be to the LORD, who has given rest to his people Israel just as he promised. Not one word has failed of all the good promises he gave through his servant Moses." (1 Kings 8:56)

—He remembered Abraham; he will remember you.
For he remembered his holy promise
    given to his servant Abraham. (Ps. 105:42)

—The divine purpose behind the Bible's promises.
Through these he has given us his very great and precious promises, so that through them you may participate in the divine nature and escape the corruption in the world caused by evil desires. (2 Pet. 1:4)

—Power promises.
Being fully persuaded that God had power to do what he had promised. (Rom. 4:21)

—God—a good Promiser.
Let us hold unswervingly to the hope we profess, for he who promised is faithful. (Heb. 10:23)

—Delays are not denials.
For the revelation awaits an appointed time; it speaks of the end and will not prove false. Though it linger, wait for it; it will certainly come and will not delay. (Hab. 2:3)

39

Running all through the Scriptures are instances of people struggling to make sense of God's delays. Take, for example, Abraham's long wait for a son. Or Joseph's extended years in prison as a victim of cruel circumstances. Or again Moses' lengthy obscurity in the desert before being called to deliver his people and lead them toward the Promised Land. The discipline of delay is written large in the life of many Bible characters, not least our Lord, who spent several silent years in the narrow streets of Nazareth. When the years speed by and something that God has promised doesn't come to pass, life can become very confusing and perplexing. We look at opportunities that are being missed and cry out: "Why? Why? Why?"

The first thing we should do when faced by a delayed promise is to check that we received a divine promise in the first place and that we are not victims of wishful thinking. Many take words from the Bible that were meant only for certain people in Scripture, apply them to themselves, and then become disappointed when those words do not come to pass. So check to see that it was a *clear promise* God gave you from his Word.

Once you are sure of this then keep in mind that God sees the end from the beginning and brings things to pass at precisely the right time. There must be no equivocation on this point, for once we question the fact of God's perfect timing we open ourselves up to all kinds of doubts. We can't stop doubt from entering our heart, of course, but we can keep it from lodging there. Whatever God has promised you (which you are sure is a promise) will come to pass. Not always in your time. But always in his.

> *Father, help me lay hold of the fact that your delays are not your denials. You have a time for everything, and I need to be patient with your patience. Hold me fast in this time of testing. For your own dear name's sake, Amen.*

WHEN GOD'S PROMISES ARE DELAYED

~

WHEN YOUR LOVE FOR
THE LORD BEGINS TO WANE

—Focus on how deeply you are loved.
How great is the love the Father has lavished on us, that we should be called children of God! And that is what we are! The reason the world does not know us is that it did not know him. (1 John 3:1)

—Allow it to grip you as it did the apostle Paul.
For Christ's love compels us, because we are convinced that one died for all, and therefore all died. (2 Cor. 5:14)

—The apostle John understood this principle too.
To him who loves us and has freed us from our sins by his blood, and has made us to be a kingdom and priests to serve his God and Father—to him be glory and power for ever and ever! Amen. (Rev. 1:5b–6)

—God loved us before, not only after, we became Christians.
But God demonstrates his own love for us in this: While we were still sinners, Christ died for us. (Rom. 5:8)

—How to deal with the sin of a left love.
If we confess our sins, he is faithful and just and will forgive us our sins and purify us from all unrighteousness. (1 John 1:9)

—The more we know the more there is to know.
And I pray that you, being rooted and established in love, may have power, together with all the saints, to grasp how wide and long and high and deep is the love of Christ, and to know this love that surpasses knowledge—that you may be filled to the measure of all the fullness of God. (Eph. 3:17b–19)

—Repentance—a must.
"Remember the height from which you have fallen! Repent and do the things you did at first. If you do not repent, I will come to you and remove your lampstand from its place." (Rev. 2:5)

It should always cause us great concern when our love for the Lord Jesus Christ diminishes and wanes. The trap we can easily fall into at such times is to try to recapture our love for him through our own energy and volition. One often hears Christians say, "My problem is that I don't love the Lord enough," and then go on to talk about trying to pump up from deep within them some enthusiasm or love for Christ. But this is not the way. Our love for Christ, we must always remember, is a response to his love for us. "We love *because* he first loved us," said the apostle John in 1 John 4:19. Our souls are designed *to respond to divine love*, not manufacture it. When we focus on how much we are loved by him, *and allow ourselves to be impacted by that fact*, it will inevitably create a response in us.

However, it must be emphasized that this principle will only work when sin has been put out of our hearts. In Revelation 2:4 our Lord says to the church in Ephesus: "I have this against you, that you have left your first love" (NKJV). Note they had not lost their love, but *left it*. There is a great difference between losing something and leaving it. When we *lose* something we usually have no idea where it is; when we *leave* something we normally know exactly where it is. We *leave* our love for Christ when we violate one or more of his commandments, and love cannot be recovered until sin is confessed and God's forgiveness is sought.

Once all is dealt with then the principle mentioned above should be followed: focus not so much on how you can love him but on his love for you. Gaze on the Cross, see love *bleeding* for you. The greater your *awareness* of how much you are loved, the greater will be your response.

> O God, I see that my love for you cannot be lost, but it
> can be left. Show me at what point I may have left it
> and help me put it right. Then teach me how to gaze
> continually at the Cross and focus more on how I am
> loved than how I can love. In Jesus' name, Amen.

WHEN YOUR LOVE FOR
THE LORD BEGINS TO WANE

_____

_____

_____

_____

_____

_____

_____

_____

_____

_____

_____

_____

_____

_____

_____

_____

_____

_____

_____

_____

_____

_____

_____

_____

_____

~

FINAL REFLECTIONS

FINAL REFLECTIONS ————

HOW TO HAVE A QUIET TIME

As a disciple, you realize that Christ must be the center of the Christian life. Spending time with Christ will help keep him at the center of your life. Many Christians testify that nothing else has been as important to them as this daily quiet time.

Set aside at least fifteen minutes each day for a quiet time. This time is an appointment to keep Jesus the center of your life. Follow the suggestions below to develop a consistent quiet time:

1. Make a personal quiet time the first priority of your day. Select a time to spend with God that fits your schedule. The morning hours are preferable, but you may want to set aside your quiet time with the Lord at some other time of the day.

2. Make preparation the night before. Set the alarm earlier to allow the time you will devote to your quiet time. If it is difficult for you to wake up in the morning, you may want to engage in other routine activities before beginning your quiet time; this way you will be alert and ready to focus. Select a place where you can be alone without interruption. The night before, gather needed materials—Bible, journal, prayer list, and pen or pencil.

3. Develop a balanced plan of Bible reading and prayer. The quiet time will help you practice the spiritual disciplines of prayer, Bible study, and worship. Read passages that relate to these subjects, and begin to write down your thoughts, feelings, and prayers in your journal. As other disciplines and ministries become important in your life, choose those subjects for your quiet time and study. Studying passages and writing down your thoughts on God, Jesus Christ, and the Holy Spirit are good ways to help you grow closer to Christ during your quiet time.

SUGGESTIONS FOR ENRICHING YOUR QUIET TIME

- Praise God for being your Lord.

- Deny yourself by confessing your sins and surrendering your will, mind, and emotions to the Master.

- Take up your cross by committing yourself to serve the Lord today, and ask him to show you how.

- In your journal, list questions for which you need answers, matters for which you need guidance, weaknesses for which you need strength, and any other life concerns about which you wish to communicate with God.

- Expect God to speak to you about matters on which he places priority and in which he is ready to reveal his will.

- Listen to God speak to you as you read his Word.

- Read the Bible systematically. A systematic study of the Bible is the best way to understand and experience God. You may want to study specific subjects, doctrines, or books of the Bible, in addition to your daily reading assignments.

- Mark words, phrases, and verses that speak to you. In the margin of your Bible, place an *M* beside verses you want to memorize; a *T* beside verses with significant teachings for your life; a *C* for correction to life's course, an *R* for training and right living, and a *W* beside a verse to be used in witnessing.

- Summarize what you believe God has said to you through Scripture. Review what you have marked. See if a pattern emerges. Has a particular word or verse spoken to you? Write in your journal what God has said to you. What response do you need to make in order to be a better disciple?

- Write in your journal your responses to God. This will document your conversations with him and help you follow your growth as a disciple.

- Review your journal regularly to see how God has answered your prayers, given you new insights, resolved difficulties for you, and drawn you closer to him.

A 52-WEEK GUIDE FOR
READING THROUGH THE BIBLE

Week 1:	Genesis 1–26	Week 31:	2 Chronicles
Week 2:	Genesis 27–50	Week 32:	Psalms 101–150
Week 3:	Matthew	Week 33:	Ezra; Nehemiah;
Week 4:	Mark		Esther
Week 5:	Exodus 1–21	Week 34:	Proverbs
Week 6:	Exodus 22–40	Week 35:	Matthew
Week 7:	Luke	Week 36:	Isaiah 1–35
Week 8:	John	Week 37:	Isaiah 36–66
Week 9:	Leviticus	Week 38:	Mark
Week 10:	Acts	Week 39:	Luke
Week 11:	Numbers 1–18	Week 40:	Jeremiah 1–29
Week 12:	Numbers 19–36	Week 41:	Jeremiah 30–52;
Week 13:	Romans; Galatians		Lamentations
Week 14:	1 & 2 Corinthians	Week 42:	John
Week 15:	Deuteronomy 1–17	Week 43:	Acts
Week 16:	Deuteronomy 18–34	Week 44:	Ezekiel 1–24
Week 17:	Ephesians;	Week 45:	Ezekiel 25–48
	Philippians;	Week 46:	Romans; Galatians
	Colossians;	Week 47:	1 & 2 Corinthians
	1 & 2 Thessalonians;	Week 48:	Daniel; Hosea;
	1 & 2 Timothy;		Joel; Amos
	Titus; Philemon	Week 49:	Ephesians;
Week 18:	Hebrews; James;		Philippians;
	1 & 2 Peter		Colossians;
Week 19:	Joshua		1 & 2 Thessalonians;
Week 20:	1, 2, & 3 John;		1 & 2 Timothy;
	Jude; Revelation		Titus; Philemon
Week 21:	Judges; Ruth	Week 50:	Obadiah; Jonah;
Week 22:	Job 1–31		Micah; Nahum;
Week 23:	Job 32–42;		Habakkuk;
	Ecclesiastes;		Zephaniah;
	Song of Solomon		Haggai; Zechariah;
Week 24:	1 Samuel		Malachi
Week 25:	2 Samuel	Week 51:	Hebrew; James;
Week 26:	Psalms 1–50		1 & 2 Peter
Week 27:	1 Kings	Week 52:	1, 2, & 3 John;
Week 28:	2 Kings		Jude; Revelation
Week 29:	Psalms 51–100		
Week 30:	1 Chronicles		

HOW TO EXPERIENCE NEW LIFE IN CHRIST

Study these Bible verses for God's Word on the subject:

1. *For all have sinned and fall short of the glory of God.* (Romans 3:23)
   Everyone is a sinner. There are no exceptions.

2. *For the wages of sin is death, but the gift of God is eternal life in Christ Jesus our Lord.* (Romans 6:23)
   Death means separation forever from God. Eternal life comes by trusting Jesus Christ.

3. *But God demonstrates his own love for us in this: While we were still sinners, Christ died for us.* (Romans 5:8)
   God loved us sinners so much that he gave his Son to die for our sins.

4. *That if you confess with your mouth, "Jesus is Lord," and believe in your heart that God raised him from the dead, you will be saved.* (Romans 10:9)
   To be born again, you must believe that Jesus died for your sins, and declare that you accept him as Savior.

5. *Everyone who calls on the name of the Lord will be saved.* (Romans 10:13)
   This is God's promise to you—that if you accept Jesus, he will accept you.

   Call upon the name of the Lord now as you pray this prayer:

   > *Dear God, I know I have sinned by breaking your laws, and I ask for your forgiveness. I believe that Jesus died for my sins. I want to be born again and receive new life in him. I will follow Jesus as my Savior and attempt to obey him in all that I do. In the name of Jesus I pray, Amen.*

To grow in your new life in Christ, read your Bible, pray, and get involved in a Bible-believing church where you live.